Kaj Munk

By the Rivers of Babylon

The Wartime Sermons

Kaj Munk

By the Rivers of Babylon

The Wartime Sermons

By the rivers of Babylon, there we sat down, yea, we wept, when we remembered Zion.
We hanged our harps upon the willows in the midst thereof.
For there they that carried us away captive required of us a song; and they that wasted us required of us mirth, saying, Sing us one of the songs of Zion.
How shall we sing the LORD's song in a strange land?

Psalm 137

New Nordic Press 2013

Copyright © 2013 by New Nordic Press
Translation © by Brian Young

No part of this book may be reproduced in any form or by any means without permission in writing from the publisher, except by a reviewer, who may quote brief passages in a review.

ISBN 978-0-9896010-0-9
LCCN 2013943150
New Nordic Press
Port Townsend, WA
www.newnordicpress.com
Cover painting by Else Young
Cover layout by Marita Sempio
Printed by Lightning Source
Printed in the United States of America

Acknowledgements

Arnold Busck published a collection of Kaj Munk's sermons in 1941. The title was "Ved Babylons Floder," (By the Rivers of Babylon). It comprised 24 sermons from 1941, the second year of the German occupation. An English translation of a selection of those sermons was made by John M. Jensen in 1945. They are no longer in print.

The project to translate and publish a new and expanded selection of Kaj Munk's wartime sermons was suggested to me by Solvej Mehring, (Kaj Munk's youngest daughter), and I thank her for that. I also want to thank my wife Else for reading my work, and for painting the cover for the book. Sister Reparata Hopp (a close friend of Lise Munk) of the Benedictine Monastery in Tucson read and commented on all twenty-five sermons, and also provided her own translation of Kaj Munk's first sermon, which is given here. Hanne Munk (Kaj Munk's daughter-in-law) suggested that I include Kaj Munk's first sermon. Its inclusion adds balance to the book. Arense Lund (Kaj Munk's granddaughter) wrote the foreword. Thanks also to Jørgen Albretsen of the Kaj Munk Research Institute at Aalborg University for providing assistance with archival documents. The photos are from the archives at the Royal Library in Copenhagen.

Brian Young

Port Townsend 2013

By the Rivers of Babylon

A foreword

My grandfather, Kaj Munk, was murdered fourteen years before I was born. But he came alive for me through reading his works, and through the many memories that my mother and grandmother had of him.

I became fascinated with him through reading his theatrical works, but I came to love him through reading his sermons. Although most of the sermons in this book were written during the war, and do speak of the need to resist the occupation, his love of mankind runs like a red thread through all of them.

In his sermon on New Year's Day, 1944, which is not really a sermon, but a speech, he says:

"I do not stand here to preach hatred against anyone. That is quite impossible for me. I don't even hate Adolf Hitler."

He could say that, even knowing that German assassins could come for him at any time. And they did a few days later. My mother, who was twelve when her father was murdered, talked about him as a family man. He played often with his children, and would tell them stories. And with my mother, Yrsa, who was the oldest of the children, he also shared his art.

He had a daily routine, where he would work on his dramatical works in the morning. Then, over a cup of coffee and honey bread, he would read aloud the morning's work for her. She was a very precocious child who could take it into her head to say; "Dad, Dad, you can't write the same thing on page twelve that you wrote on page eight."

He wrote a poem for her, in which he says:

> *You were a little girl child,*
> *So bright, and yet some mischief.*
> *With a heart so true,*
> *Of all the people it was you,*
> *Who was the poet's best friend.*
> *And from whom he learned the most.*

She missed him throughout her life, but she understood completely why he had to do what he did. She never blamed him for not having fled to Sweden to save his life.

He loved God, life, his family, and nature. Yes, he loved the whole world. He has always been a role model for me. He wrote; "Never, never, never ask if it's worth it—ask only if it's true!"

Arense Lund

Copenhagen 2013

About the sermons

Kaj Munk gave his first sermon in August of 1919 when he was still a theology student, just twenty years old. That sermon was given at Skovlænge church in the morning, and in Gurreby church in the afternoon. Both churches are close to the village of Opager where Kaj Munk spent his childhood. Although it is not one of the "Wartime Sermons," it is included here because it adds balance to the others, and because Kaj Munk's characteristic voice can be heard so clearly, even at that age. It was a voice that would be heard again so forcefully twenty years later, when Denmark was thrown into the long night of the German occupation.

The next sermon in this collection was given at Vedersø church five days after the German army invaded and occupied Denmark. That was the beginning of the long dark night of occupation, and Kaj Munk's sermons would grow increasingly critical of the German occupation. The next sermon in this collection was given just two weeks later.

The following sixteen sermons in this collection were given in 1941, and the increasing denunciation of the occupiers, and the Danish collaborators, is clearly heard. The German occupiers were at the same time becoming increasingly aware of Kaj Munk, and plans were being made to silence him. His works were censored and banned, and it became illegal to perform his plays.

The next three sermons were the famous "Underground Sermons," printed in Struer in 1943, and distributed "illegally" through the Danish underground. The first printing of 26,500 copies was on 23 May. The Germans obtained a court order for their confiscation, but only managed to get 10 copies, and later a few hundred that were taken at post offices.

Sermon 23 was given on Sunday, 29th August 1943, the day the Danish government collapsed, and the German occupiers declared martial law in all of Denmark. It was the day Kaj Munk had been waiting for, and had called for in his sermons and many articles and speeches. It was, in the words of Kaj Munk, "a proud day for Denmark."

The next sermon was given at Copenhagen Cathedral (Vor Frue Kirke) on Sunday, 5th December 1943. By that time it was illegal for Kaj Munk to preach anywhere. He had planned to give a sermon at The Church of the Holy Spirit (Helligaands Kirke) in Copenhagen, but there permission was refused, fearing possible violence and retribution from the Nazis. Munk received permission to preach at Copenhagen Cathedral from the pastor there, and that was kept a closely guarded secret so that the Gestapo could not stop him. Kaj Munk sat discretely in the audience, and at a signal from the pastor ascended to the pulpit, gave his sermon, and was then escorted quickly and safely out of the church.

At this time plans were being made at the highest level to silence Kaj Munk, as well as other leading voices in Denmark. The Danish people were in full and open revolt, and Hitler demanded that steps be taken to silence the resistance. And Kaj Munk was specifically targeted.

The last sermon in this collection is called "Kaj Munk's last sermon." It was given at Vedersø on Saturday, 1st January 1944, three days before he was murdered. This sermon was, in a sense, more like a speech to his parishioners. Kaj Munk did not wear his vestments, and did not ascend to the pulpit. He stood in front of his parishioners in his daily clothing, and opened his heart to them.

Kaj Munk did give a sermon the next day, Sunday 2nd January, at Vedersø church, but no written record or summary of that sermon has been found.

About Kaj Munk

Kaj Munk was born Kaj Harold Leininger Petersen on January 13, 1898, in the town of Maribo on the Danish island of Lolland. He lost his parents at an early age: first his father when he was just one, and then his mother when he was five. He was soon afterwards adopted by his mother's cousin Marie, and her husband Peter Munk. It was from them that he got his last name. They lived on a small farm in Opager, 15 Kilometer west of Maribo.

Kaj's new parents belonged to the "Inner Mission" or evangelical movement, and that would come to influence the young Kaj Munk. He was often present at "conversions" in the movement's Inner Mission house in Brandstrup, a neighboring village.

Marie Munk had decided early on that Kaj should study for the ministry. He was clearly a gifted child, and she thought that anything else would be too little for him. Kaj showed an aptitude for language, and was already writing poetry while still in elementary school. He would later find it difficult to choose between the two callings—poetry and the church. In the end he chose both, and became known as Denmark's pastor-poet. Yet he was perhaps best known for his theatrical works. During the thirties Kaj Munk was the most frequently staged dramatist in Scandinavia. He is perhaps best known outside of Scandinavia for his drama "The Word," which was adapted for the screen by Carl T.H. Dreyer in 1954, and filmed on location in west Jutland near Vedersø. Kaj went to high school in Nykøbing on the island of Falster. He enrolled at the University of Copenhagen in 1917 as a theology student, and graduated in 1924.

After graduation the time had come to find a position, and he applied for a post at the church in Vedersø in western Jutland. Kaj did not even know where the town was, and had to consult a map to find it. There were just six hundred souls in his new parish.

Kaj Munk gave his first sermon in Vedersø on New Year's Day, 1924. He would remain pastor at Vedersø until his death twenty years later, January 4th, 1944.

That was the day the Nazis would try to silence him. Denmark was in the fourth year of the German occupation, and in open revolt. Kaj Munk had been an outspoken critic of the German occupation, and an increasingly outspoken voice of the resistance. The Nazis had learned nothing about Denmark. They murdered Kaj Munk, but they could not silence him.

Kaj Munk was a beacon of light in Denmark's darkest hour. He is one of Denmark's most noted and discussed men of letters, and he remains so to this day. Although there was then, and continues to be to this day, controversy surrounding the life and the works of Kaj Munk, the fact that he grew progressively critical of the Nazi occupiers, that he refused to be silenced, and that he paid for that with his life, cannot be denied. After the war ended there was a scramble among many of those who were once willing lackeys of the German Reich to regain, or retain power in Denmark. Kaj Munk, who had been unwilling to compromise, was an uncomfortable thorn in the side of those who did—the collaborators. Revisionist historians, and those who preferred to cover their own tracks, tried to write him out of history. He was what we would today call an inconvenient person, who had spoken an inconvenient truth. But interest for Kaj Munk is alive, and is again growing in Denmark.

Brian Young, translator-editor

Port Townsend 2013

Kaj Munk

LIST OF SERMONS

Kaj Munk's first sermon	1
Be afraid, but not dismayed	5
Chasten us as a people	9
My Lord and My God	13
The Good Shepherd	19
A Little While	25
Sin, Righteousness and Judgment	29
Pray in the Name of Jesus	35
Ye Shall Be My Witnesses	41
The Rich Man and Lazarus	51
The Feast of the Great King	57
God's Concern for the Individual	63
Moses and Christ	69
The Call of the Apostle Peter	75

The Wrath of God	81
Faith in the Invisible	87
The Unfaithful Steward	93
The Good Samaritan	99
God and Caesar	105
Christ and John the Baptist	111
The Christ Child and Stephen	119
Christ and Denmark	125
Today is a proud day for Denmark	135
Sermon in Copenhagen Cathedral	139
Kaj Munk's Last Sermon	147
Works in English by and about Kaj Munk	155
Endnotes	157

24 August 1919
Luke 19:41-48

Kaj Munk's first sermon

When he came nearer and saw the town, he grieved over it and said: If only you knew also in this day, what serves to your freedom. But now it is hidden from your eyes.

Jesus is on the way to the capital. Let us bring the picture closer to our own life.

Straight before him lies the capital, with its many steeples towering to the clouds. But the spires of the churches are nearly hidden by the black smoke of the nearby factories. Everywhere the noise of streetcars, motorcycles, and cars is heard. Everyone seems to be seized by a feverish restlessness. And so they actually give witness to the fact that they do not know what serves to their peace.

The rich hurry past Christ in their expensive cars. They are the people who have their wealth secured, or credit in the bank. Christ has never expected anything great from the upper classes. His glance seeks the weak and forsaken, but he can no longer find them. In all eyes he reads self-conceit and defiance. Then grief seizes him. He remembers his previous words of dejection about the Son of Man: when he comes to the earth again, will he still find that faith is there? The freedom and unity he proclaimed have become capitalism's arrogant tyranny, and socialism's dictatorship of the majority. His "Do not be concerned for tomorrow" became state sponsored indolence. His command to obey Caesar out of the fear of God had become a scornful declaration by a so-called Christian people that freethinkers be appointed leaders;

His teaching of deeds of mercy and charity became sickening humanitarianism. "Love God with all your heart and your neighbor as yourself" became "Love gold with all your heart and no one like yourself." It has been said: "Strike it rich, and feather your own nest, as long as your ration-card can hold out."

What Jesus sees is a mass desertion. Society has paid official homage to his ideas and given them a fairly good day. *If you but knew in this your day, what things serve for your peace, he sighs*, but he is drowned out by the victorious sound of inventions: *We are subduing the universe with airplanes, diesel engines, and radios. What use is it to gain the whole world, yet suffer the loss of one's soul?* he replies. But no one believes him. Inventions are the human intellect's vain victory, but they may become the human soul's eternal defeat.

Jesus enters the city and stops at the temple, his own church. And what does he see there? Friction, distrust, denunciation of others, faultfinding, helplessness, and doubt. He sees that this society is rotten, its technical wonders are of use to no one, its conceited and imagined excellence is ridiculous, its whole Tower of Babel is a leaning ruin: *That day shall come upon you, when your enemies will cast a rampart up about you and besiege you round about and press you everywhere. And they shall utterly lay you waste, and your children in you, because you did not know the time of your visitation.*

But must it be like this? Must our fatherland march forward to self-destruction? We have no right to sit back; we have to know the time of our own visitation. It is today! Each one of us must say to himself that tomorrow can be too late. It is today that we must repent of our sourness, obstinacy, suspicion, weakness of will—and thinking only of oneself!

It is today that we must begin the life that is proper to a Christian, in prayer to the Lord in high heaven that He will teach us justice through mercy, to heed the number of our days, and let His wisdom rule

Sometimes it is difficult to understand or to believe that I am guilty of my own sin. Then I must rise up and smash this doubt to bits, and then I can move on. The sense of guilt is contrary to all logic, and that is exactly why it is the voice of life. To be a sinner is to be far from God, but only those who are far from God, can then be close to God. The Church's duty is to hold your sin up before your eyes, and to whisper God's merciful forgiveness in your ear. The Church can be neither Capitalism's henchman—which it has been for all too long—nor Socialism's lackey—which it now desires to be. The Church must be itself.

So severely and earnestly has God bidden me to speak in Skovlænge Church today! I was not too happy about it. Indeed, it is always easier, especially for a young person, to simply strike a well-known chord. Also, I think I am too young and inexperienced, and all too often I fail and falter. But God has given me this difficult text to base my first sermon on, and I had to obey—and I begged him to help me, and I believe He has placed His word upon my tongue.

It seems to me that we can expect hard times for this country, which our God and Father has given us in heritage. This is a time of struggle as to whether it must be blotted out and forgotten; a struggle between, on the one side, external enemies and internal subversives, and on the other side the congregation of the Church of Christ—not Grundtvigian and high church and inner-mission, or whatever they call themselves—but one great army, gathered together by the authority of Jesus Christ. A State cannot be built on technical progress, on wealth, on laws, and reforms.

All that is in itself only vanity. So says the Lord your God today through the word of the text: None can endure, who does not choose Jesus for his King. *Anyone who has lost God's Spirit must surely die, for in God's Spirit is life.*

14 April 1940, Vedersø
1st sermon after the invasion
3rd Sunday after Easter
John 14, 1-11

Be afraid, but not dismayed

(2. Chronicles 20:15)

Let not your heart be troubled: ye believe in God, believe also in me.

In my Father's house are many mansions: if it were not so, I would have told you. I go to prepare a place for you. And if I go and prepare a place for you, I will come again, and receive you unto myself; that where I am, there ye may be also. And whither I go ye know, and the way ye know. Thomas saith unto him, Lord, we know not whither thou goest; and how can we know the way? Jesus saith unto him, I am the way, the truth, and the life: no man cometh unto the Father, but by me. If ye had known me, ye should have known my Father also: and from henceforth ye know him, and have seen him.

Philip saith unto him, Lord, shew us the Father, and it sufficeth us. Jesus saith unto him, Have I been so long time with you, and yet hast thou not known me, Philip? he that hath seen me hath seen the Father; and how sayest thou then, Shew us the Father? Believest thou not that I am in the Father, and the Father in me? the words that I speak unto you I speak not of myself: but the Father that dwelleth in me, he doeth the works. Believe me that I am in the Father, and the Father in me: or else believe me for the very works' sake.

In this Sunday's Gospel, the Holy Scripture brings us a greeting from Christ. It begins in this way: *Let not your heart be troubled: ye believe in God, believe also in me.*

It is the last evening that the Saviour is together with His friends. He knows that, but they do not. By tomorrow night it will have happened, and He knows their sorrow already. They will feel as people do when they know that nothing worse could have happened to them. The despair over what they have lost will mix with shame and guilt: we could have protected Him better, it is our fault, and we should have been able to prevent this from happening to Him. Jesus sees all of this in advance, and He knows too that it is necessary that they experience this sorrow, and live through it.

But what must not happen is that they get mired in their sorrow. Christ is too dynamic a personality to endorse sorrow as something worthwhile in itself. It is a great tragedy when one feels so heartbroken that it is nearly unbearable, and that one can nearly succumb to it. That is far better than being indifferent, and frivolously avoiding anything difficult. But grief has never been a goal for Christ. Sorrow is not there for its own sake. He will use it for something.

And it is for just that reason that He is not afraid to burden His disciples with this heavy gift. He is not one who *understands* Peter when he rejects Him, or pretends not to hear, or simply turns his eyes away from His weak friend. No, he fixed His eyes upon this mumbling and stuttering man, and it was a gaze that struck deep, one that caused sorrow—and Peter went outside and cried bitterly. But from those tears over his fall grew the heart that, more than any of the others, would receive the message of the resurrection, and be so completely possessed by it, that he would accomplish that great achievement that was to be the founding of the Christian church.

Judah's despair was different. That was sorrow only felt for itself, that was wrapped up in it, and shut itself in for all time—in the grave.

Jesus was not interested in such useless sorrow. The worst that one can use their hands for is to wring them. It is for that reason that His parting words to His friends were: *Let not your heart be troubled.* That does not mean: do not be afraid! For we can all be afraid. Even Christ could be afraid. Well, there may be some who have no fear, and it's easy for them. There is really not much to thank them for. But to be able to comprehend and feel the fear within, and still, with a pounding heart, to stand fast as did Luther in Wittenberg—that is an accomplishment. One might even say that the Man in Gethsemane was more fearful then any other person had ever been. It is always a strong reaction when one sweats from fear so that drops fall to the ground. But it had never been known that the drops could be of blood. Maybe it was because He knew fear so deeply that He became that which none of the fearless ever could have become—that He became the world's Saviour.

This man could not part from His friends with a brave shout: do not be afraid! Or—have courage! It was all right for them to be afraid, as long as they did not surrender to fear, and did not get mired in their sorrow. It is for that reason that He said: *Let not your heart be troubled.* And still it was not simply a friendly wish, or a brave appeal. It was also a demand, and it was based on this: *You shall believe in God, and you shall believe in me.*

When I was a child I was told a story about my friend Martin Luther, who had once experienced a period full of worry and melancholy. His good wife Kathe, who was stronger in the feminine instincts than in the spiritual, finally decided that something had to be said. And, being a woman, she would say it with clothing. When Luther next entered the room she was sitting there dressed in black from top to toe. *But Kathe, has someone died? Yes,* she answered, *I can sense it on you, that it is the good God.*

Let not your heart be troubled: ye believe in God, believe also in me. The next day they would be standing at His grave—paralyzed, and destitute. That which had been the foundation of their lives had been taken away from under them. They felt as if they stood on thin air, like ghosts. They were no longer alive, and yet were still there. In this deep distress the word came to them, that God was not dead. On the contrary, He was alive, and active: there was a purpose to all of this—*I go to prepare a place for you, and I will come again, and receive you unto myself.*

His words helped them to endure.

28 April 1940, Them church
2nd sermon after the invasion
Hebrews 12:6

Chasten us as a people

For whom the Lord loveth he chasteneth, and scourgeth every son whom he receiveth.

Daring, daring, daring are these words: *Father, the hour has come, glorify your Son*! Daring—because He understood what He said. We would have to be almost soulless not to be shaken by those words. He understood what He had said, but His friends and companions that were with Him that last evening understood nothing.

It was a gala evening. The lamb had been slaughtered. But He knew that things could not continue in the almost carefree way that they had done so far. There would be no more walking between spring flowers and frolicking lambs in the meadows by the Sea of Galilee. No more holding an audience spellbound with powerful words and graphic images. But the disciples didn't believe Him. They had seen that He was the Son of God. Couldn't He, in the moment of catastrophe, find a way out? Could He be dragged before a court and cross-examined by the scholars? That surely could not be the way that God's Kingdom would come. But He knew that the hour had come. He saw a young man hang on a plank and die a feverish death. And it was He! And it was not something that would happen in the distant future, but tomorrow. Just tomorrow, and then there would be nothing for His friends to be together with than a poor corpse. That was what He saw when He said: *Father, glorify me!*

We love our Saviour so much because we have a God who is human, a God about whom it is told, that in the hour of fear His sweat fell like drops of blood to the earth. We are not talking about a false hero, but of a man who cringed and prayed—*Father, if it is possible, let this cup pass from me.* And He bore not just His own sorrow, but also the sorrow of His carefree friends. He knew that tomorrow they would understand nothing of this. Where was all that which they had built their lives upon? They had seen a brilliant vision; now they would look into a grave. But He would not take their sorrow from them.

And that is a point where we pastors often reproach ourselves—because we have not followed Him in this. We have heard of the pastor's comforting words at the funeral. But it's not true. Man possesses no words that can take away the sorrow we feel when we stand at the grave of one who was more beloved than ourselves. There are no comforting words when an inner voice is saying: You acted like a dirty swine, or a loathsome scoundrel, in this or that situation. We can find excuses, or explanations, but they cannot silence the inner voice. There are no such words, and if the Saviour had known any, He would not have used them. He would not take the disciples' sorrow from them. They would be left fainthearted and powerless. But He would have to do something so that when the first pangs of sorrow were over they would not retreat into themselves. To break down in despair is a sin. Sorrow is not a stage affectation for our Saviour. It is a tool in God's hands to be used for His people. The disciples would learn, in the darkness of the Easter night, that the Saviour had to be killed before He could be resurrected. The disciples had to experience this failure so that they could carry His work forward. That is why He spoke as He did. That is why He washed their feet, and gave them the mystery of the Sacrament. He planted it in their hearts, so that in the decisive moment they would burst forth upon the earth.

And then tomorrow came, and the happy, mild, and carefree Saviour was crucified. And then we saw how pitifully the disciples failed, how they ran with their tails between their legs. We saw how one of them retreated into his sorrow, and how the liveliest of them swore that he did not even know that person. That is how far they had to fall before they were fit to receive the resurrection. What would the resurrection have been without a death? The disciples thought that things would continue to get better and better, that the priests would eventually have knelt before Him, that the Romans would have left the country of their own free will, and that eternity would finally come as a seamless continuation of this joyful life on earth. This lie had to be crushed in a very brutal manner. That is how stern God would have to be. Then the disciples could receive the resurrection. But the disciples did not become gods. They kept their human weaknesses while they spread the gospel out across the earth. One of them was thrown into prison in Rome for his faith. Some friends helped him to escape, and early one morning Peter slipped out of Rome, glancing left and right to see if he had been followed. And then he saw a vision in the early dawn, a figure that he knew, who appeared before him. And he said: Lord, where goest thou? And the figure answered: I am going to Rome, to receive the crucifixion. And old Peter, who was close to seventy, turned around. He was crucified. The spineless branch, the trembling shoot, had become a rock.

Dear parishioners! The remarkable thing about this book is that it is always relevant. The things that it tells about happened 2000 years ago, but the same things are happening today. God help us, that we may understand that, and live accordingly.

Let us pray—

Give us, as a people, the rebuke that we deserve. We understand now, more than just a month ago, that You are not just present in the quiet breeze, but also in the howling storm. We had a free fatherland, and an old Christianity, but we forgot that. We set it aside like a treasure that we could always take out later. We admit now that we did not act correctly. Give it back to us, Lord, when you have changed the spirit in our hearts. Then we will be warm-hearted Danes and Christians, without hollowness and half-heartedness. Give us the cross, so that we can find resurrection as a people.

Amen!

20 April 1941
1st Sunday after Easter
John 20:19-30

My Lord and My God

Then the same day at evening, being the first day of the week, when the doors were shut where the disciples were assembled for fear of the Jews, came Jesus and stood in the midst, and saith unto them, Peace be unto you. And when he had so said, he shewed unto them his hands and his side. Then were the disciples glad, when they saw the Lord. Then said Jesus to them again, Peace be unto you: as my Father hath sent me, even so send I you. And when he had said this, he breathed on them, and saith unto them, Receive ye the Holy Ghost: Whose soever sins ye remit, they are remitted unto them; and whose soever sins ye retain, they are retained.

But Thomas, one of the twelve, called Didymus, was not with them when Jesus came. The other disciples therefore said unto him, We have seen the Lord. But he said unto them, Except I shall see in his hands the print of the nails, and put my finger into the print of the nails, and thrust my hand into his side, I will not believe.

And after eight days again his disciples were within, and Thomas with them: then came Jesus, the doors being shut, and stood in the midst, and said, Peace be unto you. Then saith he to Thomas, Reach hither thy finger, and behold my hands; and reach hither thy hand, and thrust it into my side: and be not faithless, but believing.

And Thomas answered and said unto him, My Lord and my God. Jesus saith unto him, Thomas, because thou hast seen me, thou hast believed: blessed are they that have not seen, and yet have believed.

And many other signs truly did Jesus in the presence of his disciples, which are not written in this book: But these are written, that ye might believe that Jesus is the Christ, the Son of God; and that believing ye might have life through his name.

The Doubting Thomas we call him, but is that really the right name?

A doubter is a man who does not believe in anything; but Thomas—he believes in his own good common sense. Haven't we seen him often enough in 1941, and perhaps even more often again in 1939! He will grant that Christianity has great value, but he fears that which is beyond his own understanding.

The Sermon on the Mount, Jesus' at once proud and humble ways, His heroic yet untheatrical death, this frightened man, without Socrates' bravado to lean upon, for whom this is serious and bloody reality which cannot be avoided because Duty and the Call demands it, though He says *Not my will, but thine be done.* This captivates and entices the modern Thomas.

But then we hear these unbelievable stories about water turning into wine, about a man who walks on water, about decaying bodies called forth from the grave and given back to life, about angels and spirits, and finally about the Master Himself, whose dead body takes off its clothes and folds them nicely together, and then ascends to a "Heaven" which we know cannot exist in the physical world, and then, through closed doors, appears before His disciples.

These unbelievable stories are told, and yet they demand to be believed, along with the strange notions that that three handfuls of water splashed on an infant's head will have an effect on its eternal fate, and that a piece of bread and a cup of wine can, in some cases, be both bread and wine as well as a man's body and blood, and that those who receive thereby partake of the divine nature. Our common sense tells us to assume that these are just ancient religious ideas that zealous proponents of the new religion have applied indiscriminately to their Chosen, to make Him more impressive to the hesitant and ignorant masses.

Well, 1900 years have gone by, but Thomas is still very much alive: *Except I shall see in his hands the print of the nails, and put my finger into the print of the nails, and thrust my hand into his side, I will not believe.*

And then John tells us that this actually happened. Eight days passed in which Thomas remained outside of the disciple's fold, had no part in their new faith, their enthusiasm, or their joy in victory. But on the Sunday after Easter, Jesus suddenly stood before them, alive among friends, and turned to Thomas, saying:

You rotten friend, you sick soul, you disgrace among my friends; how can you doubt so strongly, and deny so stubbornly? Hadn't I told you beforehand how it would be? Didn't you understand from all that I have done, that God was with me, and that He would never fail me? Did you never grasp even this, that my death would be my life's triumph? And was your heart and mind closed to all that I tried to share with you? Has my choice of you, and my work for you, been in vain? Then at least you should have seen, through the joy in the faces of the others, and their awakening courage, that something had happened, and that you too should have opened your frozen heart to the gushing spring. You cannot serve us as a disciple, for you are a dead weight we can no longer carry. You and your common sense must each go away from the circle of the living.

No, Jesus did not say that. He rebuked him, yes, but mildly, and He yielded to his wish, and gave him proof for the incredible.

There were many at that time that spoke like Thomas. But Pilate smiled skeptically, while Caiaphas sneered scornfully: *Except I shall see in his hands the print of the nails, and put my finger into the print of the nails, and thrust my hand into his side, I will not believe.*

But the Pilates and the Caiaphas were allowed to keep their smiles. But no Christ came to them through closed doors.

Then why did He come to Thomas? I know the answer. Because he was a disciple! Because he was devoted to the Master.

His denial was not out of hatred, ridicule, or indifference. His heartfelt desire was just to share in the joy of others, and to believe in the total and complete victory of those he loved.

But he could not. He could not. Rather than sacrifice his "common sense", he had to sacrifice the peace and joy in his heart.

We speak so often about faith, that Christianity's key word is faith. But faith is not Christianity's deepest word, although it may well be the most powerful. Christianity's deepest word is *love*. Doubt is sin, denial is sin, but sin against the Holy Spirit is a cold heart. Thomas was a doubter, he was a denier, but he was the Lord's disciple because his heart was true to that which it had once chosen, and that to which it belonged, and to that which had also chosen him. Against faith, and against hope, it remained true, and therefore he was not cast out, but received the faith that he was not able to find on his own.

But he did not receive it at once. I can see him before me during those seven days from Sunday to Sunday. They were worse than Pharaoh's seven lean years. And just as bad for all was when Catastrophe struck, when all that they knew and understood as the foundation of their lives, collapsed and was swept away. But it was ten times worse for Thomas, who saw the others saved, while he remained outside, alone, without faith. No more bitter words than these have been uttered here on Earth: *Except I shall see in his hands the print of the nails, and put my finger into the print of the nails, and thrust my hand into his side, I will not believe.*

It was just like Jesus to employ this brilliant tactic of surprise! When the hour comes, He will be there in our midst. There would be no discussion of that, and no arguments. He simply points at His side, and stretches out His hands. Nor has Thomas any need for words. He does not look for excuses, or try to defend himself: *Why did you appear before the others when I was not present? Why did they receive the faith, while I was pushed further into despair and darkness?*

My Lord and my God! That is his confession and his thanks. And that was enough. And contrary to his common sense, he feels that his doubt and his denial are sins. His voice cries out tearfully, and then turns to a cry of joy.

We hear the ice break, and the freed waves sparkle in the sun. We do not doubt that Thomas can now go forth and perform deeds that none of the others have the wisdom for.

You see, this is the Gospel for you, my Christian friend, struggling with doubt and faith, with argument and denial. This is the Gospel, which does not come to catechize, or to evangelize, or to judge, but only to listen for the beating of your heart. Does it beat for the Lord Jesus, no matter what? Because it has chosen Him, because it belongs to Him? Then be faithful! Endure! To posses the wisdom of faith is a great joy. And you are not one who has received this gift as a matter of course. But the Master has need for your Thomas mind, and you too have a place among his disciples; and you must know, that when the time comes, He will put an end to your uncertainty and your faint-heartedness. Then you will know that it is not that, which you fail to understand, that is important. Christ has had disciples for whom the words *Virgin Birth*, the *Resurrection*, and the *Sacraments*, had no meaning. But don't just stare at them until you go blind. Don't let the devil make you believe that without this understanding, you cannot be a disciple of Christ. Beware above all of such barren and morbid introspection, about whether you are a believer or not. Such thoughts lead nowhere, except downwards. But be faithful to your heart, which has made its final choice. Practice simple Christianity. Then, when the time comes, no matter how tight the doors are closed, He will appear before you, He will show you those hands, pierced through for your sake, and you will bow down and cry out, trembling with remorse and joy: *My Lord and my God.*

And when you have finally called out to Him with so great a name, then nothing will remain unintelligible. And then perhaps those things that you could not accept before will become, for your common sense, the dearest things in all of Christianity.

But our Gospel of today reaches out so much farther. It embraces many who do not even suspect that it carries a message for them. It is known that there are deniers, driven from Christianity by the false teaching of the priests, by the secular lives of Christians, by the Church's failures and sins. They deny Christ, or think they do. But He lives in their hearts' humility, and in their search for truth. And they too can experience this *Thomas week* of despair, wincing in pain over the way that Good is trampled under an iron heel, and the struggle for justice seems hopeless. And yet they are faithful, and endure. And for them, when this *Thomas week* is over, He will appear before them, as He truly is, their heart's Guest, and the final Victor over death, and its works and deeds. And then they will each in turn greet Him, saying:

My Lord and my God.

27 April 1941
2nd Sunday after Easter
John 10:11-16

The Good Shepherd

I am the good shepherd: the good shepherd giveth his life for the sheep. But he that is an hireling, and not the shepherd, whose own the sheep are not, seeth the wolf coming, and leaveth the sheep, and fleeth: and the wolf catcheth them, and scattereth the sheep. The hireling fleeth, because he is an hireling, and careth not for the sheep. I am the good shepherd, and know my sheep, and am known of mine.

As the Father knoweth me, even so know I the Father: and I lay down my life for the sheep. And other sheep I have, which are not of this fold: them also I must bring, and they shall hear my voice; and there shall be one fold, and one shepherd.

Through the ages no image has been more beloved in the Christian church than that of the Saviour as the Good Shepherd. The first artist, sitting in the catacombs while persecution ravaged the earth above, drew, with trembling strokes, the Shepherd guarding His flock. The great artists of the following centuries continued to be inspired by this image of the Good Shepherd. And in our Danish language of today there can hardly be found a more poetic word than *shepherd*. Of course, we are an agricultural nation. All of the men who have become successful in Denmark started out as shepherds on the Jutlandic heath, that is almost a given.

And it's easy to understand why we find the image of the shepherd to be so comforting. It takes us far away from the city with its noise and unrest, out to where the brook murmurs between the flowers in the meadow, while the solemn majesty of the moor rises in the background. Winter is over and spring has come upon the land.

The newborn lamb, tottering on frail legs, dancing in uncertainty's grace, with its tail wagging, finds the source of life hidden in its mother's wool, so warm and snug for little cold noses newly acquainted with this world's cold wind. See the shepherd boy with the dog lying down at his bare feet (that beautiful, intimate relationship between man and animal!), with sun and wind playing in his golden locks, dreams drifting cross his brow, while he cuts a flute from the willow by the river's bend.

Alas, this charming idyll—I almost said Paradise's meadow—has little to do with Jesus' pastoral life. Perhaps even the little shepherd boy would not recognize that description. Perhaps there is, or was (for there will soon be neither meadows, shepherd boys, nor sheep in this land), a stern farmer with a miserly wife, and perhaps the very loneliness of the goblin heaths was overwhelming—and the roads too long for short legs, and vipers lurking to strike bare feat. The mornings were ice cold; the cloudless noon stifling hot, the sheep might stray far and wide, and hide in the hollows, and the fox too dangerous for lambs. We are told about such a shepherd boy who climbed a hill and cursed God.

And when Christ took the name of *Shepherd*, it wasn't to sit for an artist with sentimental colors on his brush. For Christ, being a shepherd was deadly serious. He walks on sore and bloody feet over sharp stones to find fallen lambs, or those lost from the flock, or stuck in thorny copse. And neither night nor day does He dare take rest. And the beasts that lurk about His flock are not small fox, a danger only to the lambs, but wolves that bare their teeth to Him as well. His place of rest is not a hilltop in the moors with moss for a pillow; it is the hill of Golgotha, the place of the skull. The Easter breeze that would play about His golden locks, strikes against a crown of thorns.

I am the Good Shepherd, He says, explaining this by nothing less than giving His life for His sheep.

This is the Shepherd whom we call ours; and so it has come to pass that we belong to Him, and will hear no other voice than His. His bloody hands and feet, His wounded back, the bloody scratches upon His sweaty brow, all this tells of His love for us, about the heart that could not fail, but would rather pay whatever price than leave us at the mercy of the wolves. It is therefore that we feel that we are not alone. *Among all the world's voices, Yours alone is the one that comforts, now and through eternity.*

He is the Good Shepherd, which also means that He is the Great Shepherd. It was the ambition of this village carpenter to be the architect for all mankind, to build the church that would become the world's eternal place of refuge. This humble man, with his modest beginning in Nazareth, had such limitless plans that not even the Roman Empire could contain them. His own account of the time and place was this: *Always, until the world's end.*

Yes, when He says these words today: *And other sheep I have, which are not of this fold,* then, although it sounds of so little, it really means so much. Blicher[1] toyed with the invention of movable sheep pens. Yet that is really what Jesus did. It was in His mastery of speech that He would come upon a common, everyday thing, and see—at once it becomes an eternal and universal thing. He could stoop down at the most unlikely stone along His path, lift it in His hands, and see—it was the stone of wisdom. And then He is standing by the Sea of Galilee, and His eyes fall upon a herd of sheep in a narrow stone enclosure, and He lifts up His eyes, and He becomes the Shepherd, and the enclosure gives way, and then His flock encompasses the entire Jewish Kingdom, and then the Roman Empire, and again the enclosure gives way, and He becomes the Shepherd for all the earth's peoples, and yet again the enclosure gives way, for He is not just the Shepherd for all of the living, but also for the millions who were, and the millions yet to come, thousands of years into the future, and thousands of years into the past—all of them.

So great was His heart! The rest of us can get by with simply loving our wives and children, and a few others as well. But His love reached out with equal warmth to all mankind. He felt the call to be the Shepherd for all of us; for each one of us He gave His life.

And isn't it a great word: the Saviour of the world! Bushmen and Hottentots, Socrates and Alexander the Great, Christian XX of Denmark, soldiers fighting in Greece, and the young man standing next to me on the platform waiting for bus 15, talking with his sweetheart and swearing with every other word, the young pilots on their flights of terror over Europe, and the small children in the bomb shelters below. And it is you I will think about, no matter who you are. He is your Shepherd, His voice calls out to you, and He has given His life to save you from the wolves.

But did it make any difference? Did He really save anyone? Are we not all at the mercy of wolves today, just as helpless as in the year 30 in Palestine?

He is the Good Shepherd, He still stands before His flock, and He still wages war against the wolves, as He has waged it through the millennia. They killed Him once, and that was His holy sacrifice, the victory that laid the ground for the great congregation in Heaven with God. But here on earth He continues the struggle for His flock. There are sheep in His flock that join with the wolves, and the sign of the curse is bloody upon their brow, and the depths of perdition open beneath them. But there are also those in His flock who are filled with His spirit. As sheep circle around small lambs when the fox comes near, and stamp their hooves and face their attacker, so they too circle round the flock, take position, and would rather be torn to death than give the thief his prey. They make no negotiations with the wolf, they make no concessions, and they are not fooled when he bares his teeth and calls it a smile.

And this is how we see the martyrs in their last moments. When Nero burned them alive, when the Bolshevists stood them against the wall, they felt that the Great Shepherd had gone this way before them, and that He came to them now, to walk that path again, with them—forward to the place of death, and in to the victorious flock in the Garden of Paradise.

We can catch a glimpse of them up there, when, on rare occasion, he anoints our eyes so that we can see that high. The brilliant light shines down over eternity's infinite flock. And they are gathered there, all of them, the great white flock, the first to be persecuted together with the last, Catholics and Protestants, evangelicals and Grundtvigians[2], people who had found peace in each other's thoughts, and people who, in mistaken zeal, had abused each other for the sake of faith, the victims of the inquisition and their executioners, joyful now that they had received each other's forgiveness and sympathy. Little mutilated children jump about with all their limbs, soldiers kneel in gratitude because they have had their blood guilt washed away, the noble savage, who has now found the deepest source of truth, the sinful woman whom the Shepherd Himself had rescued from out of perdition's trap, heroes and peasants, athletes and cripples, they are all there, all of them. And the Shepherd sits on the hill of Golgotha, which is now a flowering hill of heather, and He looks out over all His flock on the meadows by the river of salvation, and then He takes up His flute, and plays that lovely verse: *One flock, and one Shepherd.*

4 May 1941
3rd Sunday after Easter
John 16:16-22

A Little While

A little while, and ye shall not see me: and again, a little while, and ye shall see me, because I go to the Father.

Then said some of his disciples among themselves, What is this that he saith unto us, A little while, and ye shall not see me: and again, a little while, and ye shall see me: and, Because I go to the Father?

They said therefore, What is this that he saith, A little while? we cannot tell what he saith.

Now Jesus knew that they were desirous to ask him, and said unto them, Do ye enquire among yourselves of that I said, A little while, and ye shall not see me: and again, a little while, and ye shall see me?

Verily, verily, I say unto you, That ye shall weep and lament, but the world shall rejoice: and ye shall be sorrowful, but your sorrow shall be turned into joy.

A woman when she is in travail hath sorrow, because her hour is come: but as soon as she is delivered of the child, she remembereth no more the anguish, for joy that a man is born into the world.

And ye now therefore have sorrow: but I will see you again, and your heart shall rejoice, and your joy no man taketh from you.

When John wrote his gospel, he had grown so old that he was beginning to get senile. So it is that much more fortunate that we get the vivid impression that, as far as the essence of the gospel goes, his memory was still fresh and young. What Jesus said and did had had such a great effect on him that it had etched itself permanently into his mind. It's only when he starts to tell about it that an old man's rambling speech shines through in his prose. Such a personal and very human trait endears the author all the more to us, and only makes him seem closer and more alive.

Today, if the text seems to be marching in place, then that is the author's style. But through the old apostle's rambling tale we hear the Master's strong and confident voice in that terse expression: *A Little While.*

The Christian religion is to a great degree grounded on realism. It is an implacable enemy of sunshine stories. Never does it underestimate the power and influence of evil. Even if it nauseates the aestheticians, and deeply offends the optimists, it still continues unrelentingly to call sin *sin*. It does not malign God's creation, but of the life that's being lived here and now, it knows of only one decisive judgement: the world is in the hands of evil. For us, who live, suffer, and struggle, there is balm in knowing that through our faith we have received a clear message. No matter what we might have to say about Christianity, we can never blame it for having painted the world more beautiful than it is.

And then we hear our Saviour's bold, calm voice: *Ye shall weep and lament, but the world shall rejoice.* Yes, that is just what happens in this sinful world. Those that belong to Him shall weep and lament. It gives a strange peace in our souls that He has foretold our fate through these eternally valid words. Then let our want and our pain increase, let us suffer our own agonies (and that can certainly happen), and suffer for all of those who have been cast out into misery. Let our travail grow until only the pain of childbirth can be its equal—our Saviour has foretold, that this is how it would be, and yes, it is a sign that we belong to Him, while the children of the world enjoy success.

Listen to what Jesus is saying to His friends on that last evening, which we also find in another place in the long speech (from which our text of today is taken). He tells them that he will go to the Father, that it is good for them that he goes away; for otherwise the *Comforter* could not come; there are many mansions in His Father's house, He goes to prepare a place for them. *This I have spoken unto you, so that ye shall have peace in me; the world is full of tribulation, but be of good cheer, for I have overcome the world.*

He is speaking about the *Catastrophe* that is known as the Crucifixion of the Innocent between two criminals. He has the bold courage of the believer, which finds meaning in the most meaningless.

This is the faith in God's omnipotence: let evil unfold in all its sick dominion, God will know how to bend this evil to serve His eternal goal.

Do we humans know how? Not at all, not at all! But Jesus has lent us His telescope, so that not even sin can hide God from us.

So powerful is the Almighty, that he can crush this curse in His hand until the quenching dew of blessing drips from it.

Be of good cheer is the cry of the Saviour. Let us take Him at His word. Let us find our peace in Him. If it were anyone else that offered us that, it would be rejected. But when it is He that speaks to us, well, then we dare to be of good cheer. We would not dare to do otherwise.

And thus shall God's will be done with all the world and us. Out of the labour pains of Hell, the joy of Heaven is born.

Do we see the distant glimmer of a world where the old is long-gone, and see that all has been made anew. Where repentance and humility dare to establish a kingdom with glory to God in the highest, peace on Earth, and good will toward men?

Or will that never come to pass here on Earth? Is it just the Earthly life, from the awakening of the first cell on the cooling crust, until it explodes against another planet, or gets crushed to death by the celestial cold— is that its entire life, that Christ sees as *a little while*, so that first in the kingdom beyond the stars it will achieve its true life?

I do not know. And I do not ask. It is enough for me that I have been put here to fight, that it may already happen down here, and that I have been given the faith to believe that it will soon happen, and whether here or there, what difference does that make? And that I can call out to myself and to everyone who suffers: *A little while, just a little while! And ye now therefore have sorrow: but I will see you again, and your heart shall rejoice, and your joy no man taketh from you.*

11 May 1941
4th Sunday after Easter
John 16:5-15

Sin, Righteousness and Judgment

But now I go my way to him that sent me; and none of you asketh me, Whither goest thou? But because I have said these things unto you, sorrow hath filled your heart. Nevertheless I tell you the truth; It is expedient for you that I go away: for if I go not away, the Comforter will not come unto you; but if I depart, I will send him unto you.

And when he is come, he will reprove the world of sin, and of righteousness, and of judgment: Of sin, because they believe not on me; Of righteousness, because I go to my Father, and ye see me no more; Of judgment, because the prince of this world is judged.

I have yet many things to say unto you, but ye cannot bear them now. Howbeit when he, the Spirit of truth, is come, he will guide you into all truth: for he shall not speak of himself; but whatsoever he shall hear, that shall he speak: and he will shew you things to come.

He shall glorify me: for he shall receive of mine, and shall shew it unto you. All things that the Father hath are mine: therefore said I, that he shall take of mine, and shall shew it unto you.

The words we hear at our baptism are called *The Renunciation and the Faith*. I renounce, which means I turn away from the devil and everything associated with him, and I believe in God the Father, and the Son, and the Holy Spirit, which all men who have joined Christ's fold have declared their faith in?

The Holy Spirit is God, and He acts in man and comes to man. *God* is a concept outside the realm of reason. Even the word God is so great that our tongue cannot say it.

He is smaller than an atom's nucleus, and larger than all the solar systems together. He is found in chaos as well as in order. He is hidden in the greatest riddle—the human mind—and yet is above and outside of it. He is everything, though evil is not within Him. We, who are dust and darkness, cannot contain any of Him, who is eternity and light. So almighty, so exalted is He, that we cannot even approach Him. To see Jehovah's face is to die. The old Jews were right, when they forbade the mention of his name.

And yet there is something within us that wants, and cannot get by with less than, some relationship with this—God. The Holy Spirit is that secret within us that drives us beyond ourselves, to a point where we do not question and do not ask about the advantages, but only where to kneel. The Holy Spirit was not born of a woman at some time in history. It is part of God's eternal being. When David sang his psalms to Him who bore His people's burdens, and disciplined them for their sins, when Lao Tzu dreamt about the power of the humble waters, or when Socrates met his demon in his consciousness' proud choice between good and evil, and even when a native kisses the earth before his fetish, then it is the Holy Spirit that fulfills man's greatest desire, and briefly lets him know that he is right in this longing, that there is a world beyond the world, and an existence higher than his own, and higher than himself. And we dare to take yet another step forward: Rafael's light and shadows, Beethoven's all-embracing power, the beauty of the acropolis—these could not be, were it not for the Holy Spirit. And it was precisely in Athens that the apostle Paul was so powerfully taken by the thought that God was an active part of history's long course that he said, *That they should seek the Lord, if haply they might feel after him, and find him, though he be not far from every one of us.*

Man gropes his way forward. And every time that we see something, or are allowed to create something on our own, there is a spark that tells us that life, no matter what else it is, that it is also holy. And then it is that the Holy Spirit whispers in our ear the name above all names: God.

And then something happened. In the midst of Man's age-long groping through the dark, it suddenly became day. The Name above all names became a Man's name. John the apostle expressed the meaning of Jesus by saying: *The Word became flesh.* Yes, the Spirit had become flesh. The Unknown and the Unrecognizable, who we know lies beyond human understanding and instinct, gave Himself to us. He continued to govern the stars, and uphold the worlds. But He also became a man. He appeared before us. He said: *You can call me Jesus.* That is the gift that enables us Christians to never tire of singing the hymn, *All by Grace.* That is the gift that He, the Lord of everything, gave to us little ones, who squirm for a few pale seconds over the sin-smitten surface of the earth. That is that gift that makes us love God. Instead of the world's confused and unclear picture of the Creator, Jesus showed us the Father, taught us God's kind heart, His goodness, and His purity. To the extent that He is relevant to us, we have found God in Jesus. He, who knows Jesus, knows enough about God to guide him through his life, his death, and to his eternal.

But how can we come to know Jesus? Is it enough to read about a dead man in an old book? No, it's not enough. The Bible by itself is as dead as a stone. Well, all books are dead. They must be read to come alive. But for the Bible to come alive, it must be not only read, and read with spirit, but it must be read with a Holy Spirit. And this Holy Spirit is not just at work in the Bible. Something happened to it when Jesus came. *It* was no longer the Holy Spirit—*He* became The Holy Spirit. After the death and resurrection of Christ, in a strange and personal way, the Holy Spirit took His place in the Church. What is His mission there? It is to keep Jesus alive among the Christians. Christ lives here on earth, not just in the stories of the four Apostles; He lives at the baptismal font, at the communion table, where the Word is spoken, where the hymns are sung, and in the words and silence of prayer. The revelation of God is not complete. For the Christian church is still growing. Branches die, new shoots grow out, there is autumn, and there is spring, and the tree's crown changes form. *I have yet many things to say unto you, but ye cannot bear them now*, Jesus told his friends that last evening; *Howbeit when he, the Spirit of truth, is come, he will guide you into all truth*. We are joyful for these words of His. Dogmas will fall, and dogmas will be born anew. Moral concepts will cross over into their opposites, and reformations and revolutions will spread across the earth and the church. It can at times confuse us, but life is always confusing. Only death is predictable, unchanged, and immutable. Let us therefore not fear when life seems troubled and in turmoil. Only where there is stagnation is there reason to be afraid. *I am the Way, and the Truth, and the Life,* Jesus said. It is so true that these three can be united, and are united in Him.

But of course this doesn't mean that as long as we make some noise and a fuss, then all is fine. There are forces at work in the world other than those of life. For Man it seems impossible to distinguish them from each other. We are so immersed in time and in sin, that even though there is no greater contradiction than life and death, they often seem to merge in our mind. We cannot grasp whether that which happens is for the sake of the one or the other. So the more important it therefore is that we have the Holy Spirit to guide us. And if John thinks about this, whether Jesus has chosen any special areas for this guidance, then he will stop at three: Sin being the first, and then righteousness, and finally judgement.

Sin? What is sin? In a Christian sense, it's not that we do things that are wrong. Sin is a condition, it is an empire, which Jesus called the kingdom of unbelief. Sin is that condition where we do not connect our lives to Christ. For all the evil that happens, we stand mired in the common guilt of unbelief. *What can I do about things that happen in the world?* We often hear this defensive voice. Well, we can all do something. It is really our spinelessness and indecisiveness that gives rise to sin, and our lack of action that allows it to grow strong.

But righteousness is not simply a matter of shaping up and doing the right thing. Righteousness is the Crucifixion of Christ. He has gone to His father, and we can no longer see Him. But we see His sacrifice. And from that sacrifice, atonement spreads out across Mankind. And therefore the word *Judgement* is not what we would expect: rather *Damnation. You have all sinned; you are all to blame that My world has become a caricature of itself. Therefore into the lake of fire with you.* But no, the judgement means, first and foremost, that the *Prince of this world* has been sentenced. And yet still he rages in his power. But his sentence has been pronounced, and they are coming, the powerful forces that will punish him— and the abyss has already opened up to receive him.

And so we pray to the Holy Spirit, that He will act faithfully amongst us, so that we can have our Saviour alive before our eyes. In the light of His presence we shall look mercilessly upon our sins, and graciously upon the judgement of God, whose name is love, and we shall receive the strength and the courage to endure, until the judgement over *the Prince of this world* has been fulfilled.

18 May 1941
5th Sunday after Easter
John 16:23-28

Pray in the Name of Jesus

And in that day ye shall ask me nothing. Verily, verily, I say unto you, Whatsoever ye shall ask the Father in my name, he will give it you.

Hitherto have ye asked nothing in my name: ask, and ye shall receive, that your joy may be full.

These things have I spoken unto you in proverbs: but the time cometh, when I shall no more speak unto you in proverbs, but I shall shew you plainly of the Father.

At that day ye shall ask in my name: and I say not unto you, that I will pray the Father for you:

For the Father himself loveth you, because ye have loved me, and have believed that I came out from God.

I came forth from the Father, and am come into the world: again, I leave the world, and go to the Father.

Pray, says Jesus. That is his short command. It can be well to remember that prayer is not given to the Christian simply as a privilege, but also as a command.

For a time will come, for most modern men at least, when they are tempted to give up on prayer. They may feel that it does not reach beyond the ceiling. Well, sometimes not even that far. But rather, their prayers seem to sink, and pull them down with them. This opens up a flood of protests; who is going to hear our prayers? God? What do we know about God? And if He is up there, how shall He, who controls the suns and governs the eternal spirits, be able to take care of my decayed tooth? How can it help to pray? Don't the laws of nature run their usual course? If germs destroy my child's lungs, can God let the child breathe without lungs? Or: I failed God; and now it pains me so that I am losing my mind; can God just give me back my peace of mind? Wouldn't it be immoral if he did? Shouldn't I be a man, and suffer the consequences of my sin? Or again: I have prayed and prayed and prayed; will my prayers ever be answered? I have gone down a blind alley—let me turn around—let me stop!

And so, in these and in many other ways, the tired heart, when preparing for prayer, will instead be distracted by such objections. But you'll be making a mistake if the tempter's whispering can make you forget your duty. Pray, says Jesus. And if you have no other reason to pray, than do so because He has commanded it, as that is reason enough for a Christian. Be therefore faithful toward Him, and be obedient to His word! Pray, and continue to pray.

Should we use just a few moments to look at your intellectual objections to prayer? You don't see any connection between the Almighty and your decayed tooth. But don't you understand, dear soul, that God is so great that everything else is as small to Him as your tooth. He spans from eternity to eternity, and for the eternal, all things are trivial. Whether it is the collapse of a world power, or blood poisoning in your little finger, they are all, when measured on that scale, the same. Christianity's paradox is that He, the Almighty, is vitally interested in every little thing, yet has a heart that cares for your entire soul, for everything in His creation. Do you begin to see now, that you belittle God, when you think that He is too great to be concerned about small things like you?

It is precisely Christianity's gift to us that we have free access to God about anything that burdens us. Let Mary pray that the canary will get better, and let the statesman pray for the victory of justice in the great confrontation between peoples. Jesus never forgot that during his childhood there could be strict butter rationing in Nazareth. So we are thankful to Him that when He was teaching the disciples His own prayer, it was not just about the great vision of the coming of God's kingdom, or about God's will being an earthly constitution in the same way that it is with the blessed in Heaven, but that in the midst of all of those high and distant concepts, He gave us these simple words: *Give us this day our daily bread.*

And then you mentioned the laws of nature. What do you know about them? You have seen the tail end of one of them. But be assured that about its head there is a halter, and its lead is in God's hand. We have so often experienced the impossible being made possible! Just to mention one: that we can be in Copenhagen, and talk with someone in America. How do you dare believe that in your wisdom you can deny that cell tissue, destroyed through years of disease, can be healed over night through one or another treatment. Haven't the words of God taught you yet, you fool, that we humans know nothing about the limits of the possible. Then at least modern science should have taught you that. And in particular, with respect to the human body, then we see one of the great mysteries of existence in the interaction of the spiritual and the material. I could give you many examples of diseases that have been cured through the spiritual intervention that we call prayer. In a Christian society it is natural that the sick should seek healing through the two paths that God has given to us: The physician, and prayer. It is a breach of duty to use just the one, and not the other.

And then you gave me an example of how your honour, and the exalted name of human dignity, were insulted by the idea that one should ask for God's forgiveness, rather than taking one's deserved punishment. But you should not determine your own punishment. Leave that to God! There is just one thing that you must understand: you have not been created just to be lost. If such a heavy burden has fallen upon you that you feel you might be crushed, then you sin by just going your way, evading God's mercy, which beyond all understanding and merit could again enable you to serve.

But then you said that your prayers were never heard. Shame on you! What do you know about that?

You prayed for your sweetheart, and didn't get her. You prayed for your husband's faithfulness, and he betrayed you. You prayed for strength against temptation, but you failed. You prayed for faith and decisiveness, yet continued to be irresolute and unsure. So my prayers were not answered, you say; and yet again I answer you: what do you know about that?

Do you know what your prayers have set in motion, on earth and in heaven? Perhaps your prayers have prepared a place for your sweetheart in heaven that is closest to yours. Perhaps your prayers have wrought out of your husband's betrayal a secret, such that you might find each other again in a much deeper love than you could have imagined, and in faithfulness forever. Perhaps your victory against temptation would have turned to arrogance, and thus to defeat, while your fall drove you into God's arms. Perhaps God has use for the seeking and anxiety that you feel, as He has in others the need for firmness and restraint. What do you know, O man? You know nothing.

Yes, one thing we do know. Jesus has told us, *Whatsoever ye shall ask the Father in my name, he will give it you.*

So now we are at the center of things. I could have saved myself the bother of discussing all of these protests; because when it comes down to it, the protests mean nothing. These protests are the child of sterility. Don't waste time refuting them. The struggle of the spirit never wins through defence. You must attack.

Have you prayed in the name of Jesus? That is, with His endorsement? So that He can stand in for your prayer?

Prayer in the name of Jesus, that is prayer according to His spirit, that is the prayer of Gethsemane. Give me this, and give me that, which I so want, though not my will, but Thine be done.

The prayer is mine; its fulfilment is the work of God.

The world has an ugly word, a grey and bitter word, and that is *to resign oneself*. Well, the world might say gloatingly, *You Christians sure can pray, but just like the rest of us, you must be prepared to resign yourselves.*

But that's a lie. There has never been a Christian who just resigned himself.

To resign oneself means to *just accept things as they are.* Cruel fate will not have it any other way, we have to accept it, and get along as well as we can.

But the Christian who prays in the name of Jesus knows, through his faith, that his prayers will be answered. He prayed that he might keep his wife, but she grew stiff in his arms, her lips turned blue, her eyes dimmed, and she was put into a coffin and buried in the earth. He knows she is lying there, decaying. And yet he does not feel disappointed or cheated. He knows that his prayers have been answered, and he knows that one day he will again hold her in his arms, where she will be his for all time. That's how stubborn Christianity is. Surely, this is the faith that has conquered the world.

Whatsoever ye shall ask the Father in my name, he will give it you. If he doesn't grant it to me in the way I had imagined when asking, then still He will grant it to me, for I have His own divine word that every prayer in the name of Jesus, will end in *The perfect joy*.

The perfect joy! Nothing can be more contrary to the idea of resignation.

Jesus ascribes this enormous importance to prayer. It gives us this power, even over the Almighty.

By submitting ourselves to Him, we make Him serve us. He, who directs the stars, lets us direct Him. *That there, and this here,* I say to Him and point, *But first and last, according to Your will.* And He nods and smiles, and prepares for me, out of the prayer I offered, the perfect joy.

This is prayer in the name of Jesus. Well, I cannot pray that way, you complain. Then pray as well as you can. Pray in your own name, until the spirit has taught you to pray in the name of Jesus. Continue to pray, no matter how poorly you think you are doing it. In plain language, stay in training! Yes, even if you feel completely lost, just remember, that what *you* feel doesn't matter. The prayer is the thing that matters. Even if you cannot follow it beyond the ceiling, it can still continue up to the stars. Don't be tempted to just give up. If nothing else can encourage you, then remember, that to pray is a command. Pray, says Jesus. Stand up, stand up on your weak knees, lift up your reluctant hands, throw your head back, and look up, all the way up, to God's radiant heaven. And then pray in the name of Jesus for everything your heart desires, pray for those you love, for your country, for your king, for Europe. Pray for those who suffer, pray for those who are evil. Pray for yourself, and pray for your prayer. And will you continue to feel just as tired and despondent? I don't think so, but even if you do, what does it matter? You might not feel that your prayer reaches its goal, even though it does anyhow.

25 May 1941
6th Sunday after Easter
John 15:26-16,4

Ye Shall Be My Witness

But when the Comforter is come, whom I will send unto you from the Father, even the Spirit of truth, which proceedeth from the Father, he shall testify of me: and ye also shall bear witness, because ye have been with me from the beginning.

These things have I spoken unto you, that ye should not be offended. They shall put you out of the synagogues: yea, the time cometh, that whosoever killeth you will think that he doeth God service. And these things will they do unto you, because they have not known the Father, nor me.

You shall be my witness, Jesus says in the text for today. Such a challenging thought, that *we* could bear witness for Him! We, who are locked within ourselves, yet are asked to witness for Him. That insignificant people like us should bear witness for the great God of life. Can we do that? Would we ever be able to do that? Never in such a way that we could declare that we had succeeded. When we settle up our accounts, then we will at best have been ineffective servants. But we can all say that we have met someone in our lives who, thankfully, has been a witness of God for us.

It is about just such a witness that I will speak about today, dear parishioners here in Vedersø, as this is the first time we are together in our House of God since I had been to Lolland for my elderly mother's funeral. We have been put here to bear witness for God, each according to their abilities and potential: some with their mouths, some with their hands, and others with both. To bear witness for God does not mean to repeat dogmas. It is not limited to just preaching. To bear witness for God is first and foremost to live in such a way that life for others is made precious, and that the good in them is strengthened. If you are standing at a casket, and the warm tears of appreciation are running down your cheek, then you are taking leave of someone who has shown you something of God. Where there is gratitude, there is also God.

With regards to my mother; she had been a witness to Christ's love for me, both with her words and her hands. All of you know that my father died when I was just a year and a half old, and my mother when I was five. But even though I was so small, she, my first mother, taught me something that I have never forgotten, something that I base my life on even today: every night, before my child's eyes closed for the night, she folded her hands over mine, and had me say a prayer that ended with: *Good night Father, good night God and Jesus, and good night all the holy little angels.* In that way I already knew, by the age of five, that we have a home two places in this world, with all that is so precious to us; up there was father, and down here was mother, and I guess I was in both places equally.

Mother died, and I was sent to live with her childless cousin, who was married to a smallholder, and lived a few miles outside of Maribo. That thread to the eternal, which my dead mother had laid in my small hands, I continued to spin on my own. By myself I added her name to my evening prayer: *Good night Father, good night Mother, good night God and Jesus, and good night all the holy little angels.* I would not say "Mother" to aunt Marie; after all, you don't forsake the dead in that way, do you? But on Christmas Eve my heart was so warmed that I suddenly burst out with: *Since you have decorated such a fine tree for me, I will certainly call you mother too!*

So then I had a mother once again. And she was so good to me, thin and frail though I was. If any of you ever get over to Maribo you will see, on the plaque over the grave of tanner Carl Immanuel Petersen, and his wife Mathilde Petersen, how clever relatives had made sure that there would be room for one more little name to be written—before the year was over they figured. But my new mother took such good care of me that after a couple of years doctor Friborg in Rødby could say: *Now I believe he's a keeper!* Mother would warm up wool covers on the stove, wrap me up in them, and carry me in to bed, and the next morning she would carry me back again, and dress me next to the warm fire in the stove. On the wall there was a picture of Vilhelm Beck*. She read the inscription for me, and I learned it at once.

> *Brothers and Sisters, now we each go our way,*
> *Father with Jesus now, happy and glad,*
> *Each their legitimate way.*

And now, when I think back on Christianity in my childhood, then it is that picture that I remember, with its evangelical feeling, happy and glad.

Mother kept me to that evening prayer that my first mother had taught me, and had me continue to go to church and Sunday school. But I can't remember that she ever threatened me with God, or ever preached to me, or ever forced me to any thing religious. I remember that everything that had to do with God seemed festive and blessed; hymns sung at Christmas, with father's favourite hymn in the lead—*Blossom like a rose garden*—meetings in the mission house or at the Lutheran missions in small homes, where I, as a nine or ten year old boy, sat up front on a Carlsberg beer crate which had also been turned upside down[3] by the meeting, and going to church in the Sunday morning sunshine among Lolland's bountiful fields.

Then it was so wonderful that even the larks would sing along with the blessed's choir: *Praise God, for He is good, and His kindness is everlasting.*

But mother also knew God as the stern Master. She had hurt her left leg when just nine, and it caused a tubercular infection. It was Doctor Hartens' reluctance to amputate that kept her from becoming a cripple. Her gratitude to him was boundless. For over twenty years she would send him two plump ducks at Martinmas, and continued doing so faithfully until his death. So she kept her leg, but at the price of pain, anxiety, sleepless nights, and wasted energy—and for both her and father the expensive trips to Copenhagen for hospital stays! She was sure that "God had a plan for her with that illness." How often she has told me that she thanked God for her bad leg. And mother was right. She would never have been the heroine she was if heroism had not been called for. Do you hear that Denmark, who has experienced April the ninth?

Well, I didn't die, and I wasn't to be spoiled. I should be hardened. So, out to move cows! Out to hoe the sugar beets! Father shook his head, as it went so poorly. *He won't be able to do anything,* he laughed. But mother said firmly, that if I didn't have a strong body, then at least I had a good head, and *that* should be used. *He shall study for the ministry*, mother said to teacher Wested. *That's a long road, Mrs. Munk; let him become a teacher. That's too little*, was the answer from the little woman's heart and lips.

The idea was crazy. My inheritance was barely over 1,000 kroner, it was far to school, our smallholding was barely 12 acres, and mother's health was poor. But mother's words were always more reliable than a note from the national bank, and father—it is to his eternal honour, that he never complained. For him it meant many more years of getting up early, feeding the horses, and setting off for the dairy, little though he was, with short arms, heavy buckets, and milk wagons higher than those we have today. It would be toil and rheumatism, and then more of the same. And did I ever hear a complaint out of him? Never!

And mother made sure it happened. "What I say will be done." Yes, I always knew where I had her. If she had been in town she would always bring home a couple pieces of candy for me. And if she had been to a party she would always wrap up half of her pastry in her handkerchief and bring it home to me. And if she had promised me a degree in theology, then she was also determined enough to make sure it happened.

I went three years in Maribo secondary school. I would get up every morning at six, and take the walk to Ryde station through Christiansen Forest to get the train to Maribo. I'd get home late, study, go to bed, and then be off again next morning. Sometimes I would run an errand to Maribo for groceries. Then mother would get up on the counter to check behind the sugar tin or peppershaker, to see if there might be a dime hidden there. "I am grateful, my father, that you were not rich."

And then I went three years in Nykøbing high school. That was my first time away from home. And it was the first faint awareness of the faith that my home placed in me who had gone away.

And then six years at the university, and the deep understanding of the joy of having one's home in the country. I was learning to appreciate that by its absence, and I understood that it was the secure foundation for everything I did.

There were letters and packages from home every single week. All the laundry, sewing, and darning, and the new clothes, a pound of butter every Wednesday, fried duck and beef steaks, pastries and cakes, and sometimes a rabbit or a pheasant. It was always the best for me. And it's not just that they would do without for my sake, but that they would take the time to pack it up and send it to me, just as regular as clockwork. And vacations! Father would be waiting at Ryde station with Ida harnessed behind the wagon, and mother waiting at home with the table decorated. And home itself welcomed me, as it was blessed from my childhood with horses and cows, dogs and cats, willow trees and fruit trees, grain and grass, eating and talking, and then to bed in the pure rough hempen sheets that smelled of Lolland's strong soil and the Baltic's fresh breeze. And letters and packages from home every week.

You little straw-thatched house under the chestnut tree, how you taught me to love all the small homes in Denmark. The best thing about you was that you weren't anything special, and that father and mother were really just like all other people. And therefore I know how you struggle and work, how you are faithful to each other, how you care about and love each other. And it is for that reason that I hate nail polish, and haughty women, and all that ostentatious bragging. But you, my little childhood home, have taught me to see the best, even the very best, in the small things.

And so the struggle led to victory, and the Bachelor of Divinity finally made his triumphal entry through Opager Forest. But my victory was a disappointment. I accepted my calling over here with you in Vedersø. Jutland was, for mother and father, a foggy and hostile concept. Jutlanders and Poles were only known as workers in the beet fields, and there was little difference between them. But the adventure opened its arms for the two little people from Lolland. Through their many trips over here they learned that even West Jutlanders are human, and they soon felt a fondness for you, both for what you are yourself, but also for your faithfulness towards their son. For a long time they managed on their own, and took care of their livestock as long as they were able. Work was always a joy for mother. I remember one night when I arrived home from Vedersø to hear singing out in the stable. The western sun fell golden across the yard, and through the windows into the cow stable. And see, there was my old white-haired mother, sitting down, milking the cows, and singing a ballad from the joy in her heart. But when they could no longer manage on their own, they were glad for Jutland's soil. And it was mother's reward that she should be able to finally close her eyes at the parish that she had fought so hard to win for me, and to feel the final caress on her cheek by the boy to whom she had given so much of her love.

So I laid her dust to rest in Lolland's heavy clay. It was hard for me to send her away; it was as if she had died a second time. I wanted so much to have kept her grave here, just outside the church door, so that every Sunday before service I could have gone out and whispered my thanks to her, and received a flower's smile to bring in with me. But father had returned in his white casket to Landet Parish[4] two years ago. Father and mother were so different, but they had been engaged eleven years, and married forty-eight, so they belonged together in death, as they had in life.

But I would miss her. How I would have liked to have kept her here for just one more summer! I could have shown her that the tea roses from the cut by the channel back home were again in bloom over here this year. I could most surely have profited from her pithy Lollandic expressions, and her quick and sharp rejoinders—old and hard of hearing that woman was, but so quick witted! I could have had tea with her, and talked about Jesus and Jørgen Hansen, seen her take to the floor in a precarious game of tag with the grandchildren, or enjoyed the expression in her clear eyes when she was honoured by a visit, received a letter, or was invited out.

Mother was, perhaps, harsh in her judgement of other people, and she might have had a dark view of life and what it meant, as well as being modest about her own abilities. But her heart was quite different. It was in her heart that she loved to be with people, it was there that she held tight to life, and it was there that she never gave up. She could be lively and talkative—about trees, flowers, birds, and animals—her eyes would sparkle at the sight of them. And she was so interested, that octogenarian, in all that we told her, or when I showed her what I had bagged while hunting, or when Lise showed her some fabric for a new dress.

In February she got gangrene in her right leg. And it was then that mother felt the time had come to die, though she didn't want to. Then I put on my vestments, and together we partook of the Saviour's body and blood, which strengthens us for the final journey. And she recited the evening prayer from my childhood:

> *Pray, O Jesus, pray for me,*
> *Pray me into Paradise;*
> *There to live and there to rest*
> *Forever happy, ever blest.*
> *Let me always love Thee well*
> *Thou who prayest well for me.*
> *God, be my friend; God, hear me pray;*
> *For Jesus' sake, Amen, I say.*

And then death approached. Evil, hideous death, one step every day: paralysis, and then unconsciousness—the wages of sin must be paid to the last penny. That, after all, is what Jesus did for us, yet still there is a price to be human.

But finally, the last tremor of the lips, a little cry, almost as of joy—a cry of surprise; and it was good, finally, to be able to pass on. And then it was over, which means that it began again, there in that other kingdom, with bird song and green leaves, with dew and golden sunshine even more beautiful than in Christian's Forest on a Whitsunday morning, when she would take her son, and a thermos of coffee, on an early morning bike ride there in the land of faith, where for us who held each other dear, in the name of Jesus, we could say: *Always another summer.*

And finally, a thank you to those home on Lolland, and to you here in Vedersø. Thanks to all who have shown mother friendship, special thanks to the girls in the parsonage who had always been so kind to her, and thanks to Viggo, who rang the bells as we carried out the casket so that our old church could follow mother out of the parish with it blessing.

15 June 1941
1st Sunday after Trinity
Luke 16:19-31

The Rich Man and Lazarus

Now there was a certain rich man, which was clothed in purple and fine linen, and fared sumptuously every day: and there was a certain beggar named Lazarus which was laid at his gate, full of sores, and desiring to be fed with the crumbs that fell from the rich man's table; yea, moreover the dogs came and licked his sores. And it came to pass, that the beggar died, and was carried by the angels into Abraham's bosom: the rich man also died, and was buried. And in Hell he lift up his eyes, being in torments, and seeth Abraham afar off, and Lazarus in his bosom. And he cried and said, Father Abraham, have mercy on me, and send Lazarus, that he may dip the tip of his finger in water, and cool my tongue; for I am tormented in this flame. But Abraham said, Son, remember that thou in thy lifetime receivedst thy good things, and likewise Lazarus evil things: but now he is comforted, and thou art tormented. And beside all this, between us and you there is a great gulf fixed: so that they which would pass from hence to you cannot, neither can they pass to us, that would come from thence. Then he said, I pray thee therefore, father, that thou wouldest send him to my father's house: for I have five brethren; that he may testify unto them, lest they also come into this place of torment. Abraham saith unto him, They have Moses and the prophets; let them hear them. And he said, Nay, father Abraham: but if one went unto them from the dead, they will repent. And he said unto him, If they hear not Moses and the prophets, neither will they be persuaded, though one rose from the dead.

This year, the first Sunday after Trinity falls on the day of one of our nation's big festivals, Valdemar's

Day, our national Flag Day. If that hadn't been the case, would it then have been reasonable, based on today's text, to have talked about planned economy as seen through the eyes of Jesus Christ. We will have to save that question for another time. Today it is impossible not to be thinking about the fatherland. Does the Gospel say anything to us about Denmark? Or do we again need to have a pastor to cleverly tell us what to believe, rather than explaining what was said, and thus bringing the ancient Word to life?

I will tell you honestly, that I do not have to be clever, because the Lord's words are always relevant; they are always living, and always within your grasp. No matter what is in your heart, you will never find simple platitudes.

It is as if there is something taunting my people and me in this parable of the rich man. This man, who dressed up in a purple robe and expensive linen, and lived every day in bliss and luxury, what was wrong with that? That story doesn't mean that Christ wanted to get rid of wealth. He wasn't simply a boor from the countryside without any appreciation for the benefits that wealth can make possible. We know that He admired good architecture, that He visited the homes of the wealthy, that He liked it when people admired Him, and that He liked good food, parties, and was always well dressed. It was not wealth that He was against. It was the sterile, heartless, and irresponsible form of wealth that He was against. The sight of that type of wealth could turn Him into a communist. But those property owners who understood that ownership was also a responsibility, He called friends.

So let us turn our eyes upon our own people. Have we been a people of many Lazaruses? Not at all! We have known a bit about crises, and we have whined pitifully, as often happens with the wealthy when they think they're not earning enough. We have had plenty to enjoy and consume, all of us. And if we haven't actually dressed up in purple and costly linen, then have we not dressed ourselves up all the more in Fords and Chevrolets?

We have belonged, in other words, to a high degree among the owning class. And how about the feeling that owning is also an obligation? Let it be said once again, in plain words: the Danish people have been a silly and superficial people. Yes, we have been silly and superficial. A lot of good things can be said about us, but sometimes this too must be said. Don't let the words of the Prophet drown in the words of the toastmasters. We have played ourselves away from the serious realities of life. The great calls lie outside our door: the call for the fear of God, for self-discipline, and the willingness to sacrifice for our country. But we let them lie, like filthy Lazuruses, whose sores the dogs would lick. We turned to our lives again, in pleasure and folly. It'll last for our lifetime, and the devil can worry about the rest!

The rich man died, was buried, and woke up in the kingdom of death, and he was in pain.

It is almost beyond understanding, and just as hard to say, but that is what happened to us. The fools were wrong in thinking that all would be fine during our lifetime. But things have not remained fine during our lifetime.

He opened his eyes in the kingdom of death, and he was in pain.

Dear Christian parishioners, let us linger for a while with that word—*pain*. It is a raw and ugly word. *Pain*, it's a bit philosophical, romantic if one can say that, almost a fine word, and a bright word in the cold for great minds to ponder. But *pain*, it is just that, and it hurts, and continues to hurt, and oh, so hopeless it is. None of us want to feel pain, none. But still….still….

When I ask myself how it might come about, that my people might be awakened, then I wonder if there can be any other way, except through pain. And yet I think that I am beginning to sense, out among the people, a growing realization of this. "We flew too high," we say in plain Danish. But there are still so many people in this country who think that pain is when the trains don't run anymore, or the cars are blocked up, or the coffee has been replaced with a foul tasting substitute.

And so we can read war stories about how others are suffering. That is almost the worst of it all. We enjoy the collapse of France, right to the last good cigar. We read about, and admire, the Finn's hopeless struggle against an overwhelming power, while for our own land we have been unwilling to lift a finger in its honour, except to cross ourselves at the very thought.

The rich man has gotten a telescope so that he can study Lazarus outside his gate.

He opened his eyes in the kingdom of death, and he was in pain. And it wasn't some kind of *fine* pain. It wasn't doubt, temptation, remorse, or some other spiritual inconvenience. It was raw corporal pain. In plain words: it was thirst. The big binge was over. It was the next day. *Father Abraham, have mercy on me, send Lazarus, let him dip his finger in water and quench my thirst, for I am in anguish in these flames.*

Who would have thought that this champagne drinker would ever beg for water, even for a single drop that could lie on Lazarus' black finger?

And what is awaiting our people in the future? Not just a guilty conscience, or the trials of conversion— not just headaches, but stomach-aches?

Can we avoid that? Can we get our act together? Should we pray for a new Awakener in Denmark? What does the Spirit say to us? You have Grundtvig, and you have Vilhelm Beck, and you have great men of learning as few other people in the world. If you do not believe them, then I don't think you will believe another, even if I could bring him forth among you.

So we must admit that the Spirit is correct. We have heard the message so often, with such warmth, and with such authority, that we can never complain that we did not know better. We must, in other words, lie in the bed that we have made.

For we have gambled with all of life's values, we have struck the word *Holy* from our language. Our churches are empty; we have allowed our pastors to speak to us without fire in their words. We didn't know that we had a fatherland. We called them idiots, those who thought that life meant sacrifice. And we thought that instead of fighting, we could get by with debating.

Oh Lord, the measure of our sins is great.

Has the Gospel no words of comfort for us today?

No, it has none. It is that stern. If there is any comfort, then it is in its silence, that it is silent about the rich man's eternal fate.

Did he remain in the kingdom of death, in eternal pain? Nothing has been said about that.

And so it is now with this stifling ignorance and fear for Denmark: is it death, irrevocable death this time, or is there the possibility of a resurrection?

We do not know. And that is the crushing anxiety for this generation of Danes.

We do not know. But as people of faith, we know, that we cannot count on the possibility of a resurrection.

The Holy Spirit will bring to life the most powerful words from both the old and the new testaments.

"For God, all things are possible." Here it is the stamina and faith of the saints. *Seek and ye shall find, pray and it will be given, knock and the door will be opened. Where can I escape from your presence? If I ascend to Heaven, you are there, if I lie down in the kingdom of death, you are there; if I take to the wings of dawn, I would fly to the farthest sea, but there too your hand will find me, and you will hold me tight.*

We pray that these words may also apply to our precious fatherland. We do not have the courage to pray for pain. And yet we pray that here, in the kingdom of death, we might experience that which might change us, so that God might again have mercy on us, so that a new spirit can inhabit our ancient people, and that we can be lifted up from our graves to a new birth, to a new life.

It is Valdemar's Day[5], and Dannebrog is flying over our land. On this day, 722 years ago, in a single moment, when it was a matter of life and death for the King and the army, it came to us from Heaven. And for over 700 years we have turned our eyes to heaven. Now that we are again in this deep valley, may it signal us to wake up to life! May its white sign of sacrifice purge our blood, so that it again is healthy and red!

22 June 1941
2nd Sunday after Trinity
Luke 14:16-24

The Feast of the Great King

Then he said unto him, A certain man made a great supper; and bade many: and sent forth his servant at supper time to say to them that were bidden, Come; for all things are now ready. And they all with one consent began to make excuse. The first said unto him, I have bought a piece of ground, and I must needs go and see it; I pray thee have me excused. And another said, I have bought five yoke of oxen, and I go to prove them; I pray thee have me excused. And another said, I have married a wife, and therefore I cannot come. So that servant came, and told his lord these things. Then the master of the house being angry said to his servant, Go out quickly into the streets and lanes of the city, and bring in hither the poor, and the maimed, and the halt, and the blind. And the servant said, Lord, it is done as thou hast commanded, and yet there is room. And the lord said unto the servant, Go out into the highways and hedges, and compel them to come in, that my house may be filled. For I say unto you, that none of those men which were bidden shall taste of my supper.

Jesus has shown us many different images for what it can mean to become a Christian. He might see it as something as active as working in a vineyard, or as passive as a lamb resting in the shepherd's lap. In today's text he describes it as partaking of a great feast. Those who think of Christians as cynical and sulky are very mistaken. We would be some miserable Christians if we had not, at times, felt that it was a wonderful thing we have been called to. The feast of the great King, the perfect joy that God's children have felt through the ages, as their fate, and especially that of the martyrs, when their bones were broken in the lion's jaws, or their skin singed in the flames for God's honor.

Jesus calls Himself the Host for the great King's feast, but those who are invited would rather have their own private feast. They are very polite, but oh so busy—I ask you, please excuse me. The old Christian Europe has no time to take care of its Christianity. It has bought land; it has acquired colonies that it has to see to. It has bought itself five oxen—well, now it's a new kind of oxen—armoured tanks, and bombers. Or else they say: I have taken a wife—well, that was before, now they say: I have to get a divorce, then I'll be getting a new wife, thank you very much.

The people of our time would rather throw their own parties instead of attending a spiritual festival. They will create their own happiness through capitalism and eroticism. And how has it gone with this happiness? Let's speak plainly: At no time in human history have people been unhappier. The heaven that we would create for ourselves has become a hell. We spurned the great King's feast, and gone to our own, and I can tell you, it has been some party!

The uninhibited worship of capitalism has led to war—by all against all. The property owners used every means to keep all others down, and they in turn have joined together so that they too can become owners. To increase the wealth of the white kingdom, the world's coloured peoples have been harnessed to work for them. Our peace has required the oppression of the world, and internal conflict between ourselves. If you have the guts for it, just let your breath out in desperation: For now we have finally gotten an honest war. Our ideal was Humanity, but our practice was Money.

But no matter how much of a threat materialism has been to our happiness, even our existence, then the senseless worship of eroticism has been even more destructive to our domestic life. In the old days parents would decide who should have each other, and it was taken for granted that marriage was a contract for life. That seems barbaric to us today. But who can say that today's problems have been solved any better? The purpose of establishing these new relationships is to promote the happiness of the individual, and yet the unhappiness of the individual could not be greater. One talks about unlucky love in times gone by. But we have abolished love, and only unhappiness remains.

The believer is dependent on something higher than himself. But the secular man is dependent only on consideration of himself. But Man is blind. He will climb to the mountaintops, only to fall into an abyss.

But haven't we all felt moved when the romantic poets described the despair felt when two lovers could not have each other? Of course! But democracy has here, as in other places, lowered itself with its doctrine of equality for all. For they were the chosen and the individuals who had found great love. But now all will find it. Mr. and Mrs. Hansen have now been married for 23 years, and then suddenly the great love comes along, and it demands respect no matter what. Those 23 years are gone, the home is gone, the children, the self-respect, and respect for the vow made at the Lord's altar. And there is always some foolish pastor who is ready to make a mockery of his own religion by accepting Mr. Hansen's new vow of eternal allegiance to his new partner, before the same altar. And now that Mr. Hansen is at it: who knows—if he can afford it, the great love might come along again for the third or even fourth time? And the pastor is still there, cooperative, and willing to serve, and thus makes a fool of life, death, and eternity. What did we make the civil wedding ceremony for, if not for just such cases?

Let the actors, whose trade is the *great love*, and the few and the chosen, be the exceptions that confirm the rule. But for the sake of mankind, do not let artists be the examples to be followed by the general population, and for God's sake, never let the *chosen* be seen as role models. King Solomon would cut a sorry figure as a hatter, and as far as Jørgen goes, he should stay out of the castle.

Does this mean that divorce under any circumstances is reprehensible for ordinary people? Let's refrain from getting into this nonsense, and just say clearly, and without hesitation—yes. There *can* be circumstances where marriage has become so difficult that it becomes a parody. All right then, let the divorce take place, but as something to be ashamed of. He has not been able to fulfil his vow, and he leaves the field beaten. But instead we see in this shameless generation that new conquests just puff one up, and divorce is seen as interesting. It doesn't bother him, being a wretch, who has exchanged his deepest feelings and most intimate experiences with a new liaison, and broken his life's holiest vow. It doesn't bother him that his home has been broken into pieces, and that his children have felt their foundation ripped out from under them, as if a bomb had fallen, and that these children are neglected, that a woman now has the brand *rejected* burned into her body and her name, that the country has gotten one more broken home—nothing bothers him, no. He has had his passions quenched, and chosen a possibly random and short-lived infatuation for his great feelings, and just carries on in shamelessness, with his head held high.

But what if it *was* the true love, or at least the one great love?

Nothing bad can be said about true love! Nor about great love! But it is an open water fish, and is not found in rivers or lakes. It lives on the pure water we call tears. Its greatness is that it doesn't avoid such fine company as *sacrifice* or *loss*. True love is there for its own sake, and not just for its own satisfaction. It can be found in marriage, and there it is a wonder to behold, a costly treasure. But just as often it is found outside marriage, and woe be to the person who will not pay the price. And if it is so powerful that it demands all—well, marriage cannot be broken, so then it must live outside of marriage. And if it is that strong, then it must also have enough strength to live outside of marriage.

But the small love is made for all ordinary people, and the name of love is Holy, whether it is great or small. Even the small love is God's gift, God's good and blessed gift. And if you accept this gift, and take care of it, then it will survive the crises, and keep two people happy and thankful for each other. It will build a healthy and solid home for them and their children, and become one of the many small foundation stones that a nation rests upon.

Then the master became angry, scripture says. We Christians believe that it is the master's anger that we see in everything that happens to us. We believe that judgment is upon the world that was invited to God's feast, but preferred to have its own party in the streets. We hope that a new world order will lift up its head from out this woe, and that the old gods, warfare, and carnal lust will be abolished, and a simpler time will come. That social justice will eliminate the division between classes and races, and that true love, with healthy homes and happy children, and with faith as the foundation of the home, shall create a strong society, and give support to man, instead of the disintegration and chaos which is now a cultural nightmare.

And where will such a change come from? Only from one place, from the living God! Christians will eventually turn away from their egos, and hear His invitation to God's feast. In other words: they will begin to take their Christianity seriously.

29 June 1941
3rd Sunday after Trinity
Luke 15: 1-10

God's Concern for the Individual

Now all the publicans and sinners were drawing near unto him to hear him. And both the Pharisees and the scribes murmured, saying, This man receiveth sinners, and eateth with them.

And he spake unto them this parable, saying, What man of you, having a hundred sheep, and having lost one of them, doth not leave the ninety and nine in the wilderness, and go after that which is lost, until he find it? And when he hath found it, he layeth it on his shoulders, rejoicing. And when he cometh home, he calleth together his friends and neighbors, saying unto them, Rejoice with me, for I have found my sheep which was lost. I say unto you, that even so there shall be joy in heaven over one sinner that repenteth, more than over ninety and nine righteous persons, who need no repentance.

Or what woman having ten pieces of silver, if she lose one piece, doth not light a lamp, and sweep the house, and seek diligently until she find it? And when she hath found it, she calleth together her friends and her neighbors, saying, Rejoice with me, for I have found the piece which I had lost. Even so, I say unto you, there is joy in the presence of the angels of God over one sinner that repenteth.

He might not have been more than three years old when he experienced it. And perhaps it had burned itself into his mind, because he was not used to seeing his mother so nervous. His dear little mother, the anchor point in his life, behind whose skirts he could always find shelter from the world's storms! But now her hands trembled, and the few pieces of furniture in the little room in Nazareth were turned upside down. She blew on an ember in the fireplace, and lit a candle, so she could see into the corners again, saying *You haven't taken it, Jesus?* And *I just don't understand, I just don't—* and *didn't you see it, boy, I just put it down?* But Jesus had not seen anything, and was too little to understand. And then something sparkled in the light, and he heard a cry of joy from his mother: *There it is, there it is*! Voices could be heard from outside; it was a couple of neighbour ladies, who had been to the well for water, and Marie went to the door to tell about this latest sensation in world history, that a Drachma had gone missing from the housekeeping allowance, and oh how she had searched for it! And she had been afraid that Joseph would come home before she found it! But look, she held it in her hand, and now that crack in the floor would get fixed, that was the least to expect, for why else would you have a carpenter for a husband? And the neighbours had to come in to see the crack in the floor, and the Drachma again as well, and then have a cup of coffee—we might as well call it that, what they drank in those days, the same as we drink today.

But when the boy grew up he could better understand why this little episode had burned itself into his mind. It wasn't just because his mother's fingers trembled; it was more because—though he didn't understand it at the time—that it told about someone who was much larger than his little mother; It told about his heavenly Father, about the Almighty God, that even His hands could tremble over something that, in the world's eyes, seems just a tiny loss, the loss of one soul—my, my, aren't there people enough? It's crawling with them, and the problem is more about how we can get rid of them! Lances, chariots, and warships, we have to save them, as they cost a lot of money and work, but a man? He can be made for free. A man is just about the only thing that doesn't cost anything.

And it came to pass in those days, that there went out a decree from Caesar Augustus, that all the world should be taxed. That's how the Gospel begins. It was into this world, where people are abused as statistics, that the Son of Man was born.

It is a blessing to go into the Christian church and find out that while Caesar considers men objects, He, who is the Caesar over all Caesars, sees man as a goal in and of himself.

Of course, the words of Jesus are madness. What, after all, is a man? The result of sublime love at the height of its happiness and beauty? Or, perhaps, it is the consequence of a rapist succumbing to some kind of perverse drive. And see how the ditch is running over with frog eggs, and how the sun bakes it, and the water evaporates, leaving behind a dried black crust of desiccated life. Is a man more than a tadpole? Who dares to believe in the individual's value beyond being some measly pawn in a game, a cog in the machinery? But Jesus is not swayed by what the eye sees, or experience shows, or what the world's wisdom reveals. He has the insane courage to believe what God says to him. When he had gone to the mountains, in loneliness and the still of the night, He heard the eternal voice: *Can you remember from your childhood, when your mother searched for the lost Drachma? There, you have my heart for every single human soul!*

There are many for whom this seems like hopeless madness, and they give up at the start. And then they accept an even more hopeless madness, in believing that the world is as it appears.

But there are others who feel so drawn and inspired by Jesus' courage to believe in the independent reality, that they cannot do otherwise than to surrender to His courage. They think that they have never seen anything more beautiful than this daring ability to see the eternal in the most insignificant events in daily life. They listen to everything He says, as if it was a matter of life and death. He turns them into believers, and then it *does* become a matter of life and death. So it's not a H.C. Andersen story, a fable—wise and profound, rich and beautiful, with artistic truth. And how much truer it is will be up to each individual to decide. But it is the truth itself that comes through the words of Jesus. It is the truth, that there is a Lord over all things, and this Lord loves all of his creations. He guides the Sun in its course, yet follows every grain of dust on the smallest of his worlds. Yes, He is such a great Lord that for Him the smallest grain of dust is as a planet. The confused soul that turns away from Him—that lives without ideals, or what is even worse, in sin—and who holds ideals that go against His, is a source of pain and sorrow for Him. And when such a one finds his way back to Him, He rejoices, and not even the praise of the angels can bring Him greater joy.

It is a dizzying thought that I might cause God grief, or that I might cause God to rejoice!

I—God?

Either this is the height of madness, or it is the madness that we call the truth.

It is great enough to be that truth, and Jesus has assured us that it is.

And it has strengthened His disciples through all time, and shown them the way to a noble life. Wherever they went, they felt that their Father's eyes were upon them. And that gave them the strength to be faithful, and it helped them, if they failed, to find their way back again.

When the blind stoned Stefan to death, he saw the heavens open, and the Son of Man standing at God's right hand.

When Martin Luther stood against the great powers in Worms[6], he knew that God was standing behind him.

> *And though they take our life,*
> *Goods, honour, child and wife,*
> *And go forth as in God's name,*
> *Thereby is nothing gained,*
> *As God's kingdom we retain.*

When General Booth, the founder of The Salvation Army, drove the reluctant to the bench of penitence, he opened Heaven over them, so that they saw God in Heaven bend down to hear their confession of sin.

The individual's inherent divine value—that is the belief of Jesus.

Thus it is in His spirit, all that which is done to keep and protect us. The great system that we have to protect the individual is in accordance with good Christian principles. We have given God joy with our care for the elderly, the poor, the sick, for criminals, and for the mentally ill.

And we cause Him sorrow, when this work, and this care, is overdone and abused, and in that way, being discredited, works contrary to its purpose.

He who cheats to get disability payments, or is dishonest in receiving unemployment benefits, violates the spirit of caregiving to the same degree as the men who are responsible for so many of society's unbearable conditions, and do not use their abilities and power to change them.

We are responsible to God, even in the smallest things. Christians do not live under a closed sky. Through two thousand years they have lifted their eyes to see heaven open above them, and they have felt close to God.

And what about us assembled here today? What do we see? Do we lift our eyes on this beautiful summer day and see God's glory, and the Son of man standing at His right hand?

We know, that in other places under heaven, the great machines are on the move, set upon their deadly course, bearing their cargo to burn cities, and make voices cry out in terror.

Yes, but all of that which we call blood and fire and injustice, Jesus has seen, as well as we have. That is no modern invention; it is as old as sin itself.

But we pray to Jesus, that He may lend us His eyes, so that we may see that which He saw.

God's faithfulness to the individual soul!

His sorrow over sin, over all that is in my heart, whereby I too share the guilt for all the evil in the world.

Lord, share your sorrow with us, and make us pure in sorrow over ourselves, that there may again be joy in heaven and on earth.

God's faithfulness to the individual soul!

His joy over each one who finds the way to His heart!

Because He is the woman who never stops searching for that lost Drachma, and He is the shepherd who wanders into the desert to seek the lost lamb.

So there is more to see than warplanes when we lift our eyes toward heaven. We also see a God up there, heaven and earth's Almighty, whose heart does not let Him sit at ease on that Holy throne. On quick feet he descends, and wanders about, where savagery and death reign. He comforts the crying women; He lifts the broken children to His bosom.

Thank you, Lord Jesus, that you have given us faith in the unbelievable.

6 July 1941
4th Sunday after Trinity
Luke 6:36-42

Moses and Christ

Be ye therefore merciful, as your Father also is merciful. Judge not, and ye shall not be judged: condemn not, and ye shall not be condemned: forgive, and ye shall be forgiven: Give, and it shall be given unto you; good measure, pressed down, and shaken together, and running over, shall men give into your bosom. For with the same measure that ye mete withal it shall be measured to you again.

And he spake a parable unto them, Can the blind lead the blind? shall they not both fall into the ditch? The disciple is not above his master: but every one that is perfect shall be as his master. And why beholdest thou the mote that is in thy brother's eye, but perceivest not the beam that is in thine own eye? Either how canst thou say to thy brother, Brother, let me pull out the mote that is in thine eye, when thou thyself beholdest not the beam that is in thine own eye? Thou hypocrite, cast out first the beam out of thine own eye, and then shalt thou see clearly to pull out the mote that is in thy brother's eye.

The Bible tells us that there are two people who have spoken with God, as one person speaks with another.

The first one—maybe it was just an ant, but let's say it was a man. Perhaps his name was Hammurabi, but we'll call him Moses. It was he, who brought human society from heaven down to earth.

He would establish a kingdom on earth, a kingdom of law.

He would break the law of the jungle with his powerful edict: *Thou shalt not.* Thou shalt not lie. Thou shalt not commit adultery. Thou shalt not steal. Thou shalt not kill.

With majesty and frightening realism, the second Book of Moses tells us of the fateful days when the law was made.

Who can ever forget, when once having heard it, about Moses' meeting with Jehovah in the clouds and thunder of the volcano?

And Moses had to cover his eyes when God appeared, because no man can bear to see the face of God.

And yet Moses' face beamed so brightly when he descended from his meeting with God—the source of all inspiration—that the people could not bear to look upon it. He had to put a veil over it.

And who can ever forget that while he, the chosen one out of the chosen people, created his great work up there in the lonely shadow of the Almighty, the people down here had found a golden calf to dance before.

And when he came down from the mountain, redeemed and happy, the sound of that joyful music met his ears. Then he smashed the tablets that had the words of God upon them. And the punishment came, death came, remorse came, God's mercy came. And the act was repeated, and again God's fingers wrote: *Thou shalt not.*

The kingdom was established, the kingdom of the law. And the struggle continued, to make from creatures of the jungle, men in a society.

Moses, the man of God, never reached the Promised Land. He only managed to glimpse into it before his bones were laid to rest in an unknown grave.

And centuries passed. And again a man was born who would come to talk with God—Jesus.

And He too would establish a kingdom on earth. Establish it upon that which he brought down from heaven.

A kingdom of love! Established not on God's justice, but on God's mercy.

And for Jesus it wasn't enough with the words: *Thou shalt not.* Other words were needed.

There must also be a: *Thou shalt.*

And the greatest *Thou shalt* of all: Thou shalt love. Thou shalt Love the Lord God with all thy heart, and love thy neighbour as thyself. It is not enough that beasts become men. We must go further, they must become angels.

Moses saw God from the back, but Jesus saw Him face to face.

We saw His glory, the disciples said later, a glory that no one but God's only begotten Son could have from His Father, full of grace and truth.

Moses only saw God when He turned His back to him. Jesus saw Him from the front, His smile and His breast, the place of His heart.

And how has it gone with these two founders of the great Kingdom? Have they been successful? So many years have gone by that we think an accounting can be made.

It was Aaron, Moses' brother, who the people had talked into making the golden calf. Moses' fame has overshadowed Aaron's, but in reality, Aaron cannot complain about standing in his brother's shadow.

Through the millennia they have danced the Cancan with our spinning planet, and the dance around the golden calf has kept beat.

The law of the jungle has been stronger than we would have thought.

Ask down through the ages: Who has been the greatest among men today? It is always he who has been the best at lying, at whoring, at stealing, and at killing.

And yet, Moses' life was not in vain.

For they have learned from his discipline: They have organised their lying and killing, and become much more effective than they had been before in the jungle.

And if that is what has happened with Moses' kingdom, how much more hopeless can we fear it might have gone with the kingdom of Jesus?

If His goals had been greater than those of Moses, then it must have gone that much worse for Him.

The survival instinct turned its furious face toward Him.

Love? We have no need for love. In this world it is necessary to take care of oneself. He betrays life, so give Him death. And they gave Him death.

All of them!

They asked the lawyers, and they looked in the law books and nodded their heads. The priests and the soldiers, the cultured and the man in the street, an entire populace in agreement—that rare and beautiful unity: Crucify Him!

And He prayed—*Father, forgive them, for they know not what they do.* And that is why He arose from the dead.

Because His *Kingdom of love on earth* wasn't just an idea that He was proposing, or a theory that He was bandying about, or getting a degree in. It was something that He had received from God, and it was God Himself, and He paid for it with His life. That is why!

So the world was confronted by this most unnatural idea, and tried with all of its jungle instincts not to crush it.

Instead, the world tried to poison it!

It tried to lure it into the service of the forces of the jungle, threaten it to bless hatred, and fool it into dancing around the golden calf.

Or noble insanity tried to undermine one kingdom with another, to ridicule the kingdom of love with the law, and the kingdom of the law with mercy.

Moses and Jesus—two deeply tragic figures—the one more tragic than the other.

So it can be brutally said: they were made a fool of.

And yet they are the only two whose names still shine like stars over mankind today.

Because of them, the name Mankind is still a noble name. It can happen to the beasts of the jungle, that one night they hear a sound in the forest. Some of them lift their heads and listen. It is the distant morning song of the stars.

And among us there are beasts whose hearts tremble in such great longing, that the smile dies on our lips, the smile over the lyrics of the morning song of the stars.

But we know that this is impossible. We know that for sure. And yet that sound is so great that we believe in the impossible anyway.

That there is someone, and that there always *will* be someone, as until now there always *has* been someone, though there are ever so few down here in the jungle, in who that song of the morning star lives, and the struggle and the hope continue, so that we believe that it will happen again.

The great *Thou shalt not* will make us human, and the even greater *Thou shalt* will complete the work of the law.

13 July 1941
5th Sunday after Trinity
Luke 5:1-11

The Call of the Apostle Peter

And it came to pass, as the people pressed upon him to hear the word of God, he stood by the lake of Gennesaret, and saw two ships standing by the lake: but the fishermen were gone out of them, and were washing their nets. And he entered into one of the ships, which was Simon's, and prayed him that he would thrust out a little from the land. And he sat down, and taught the people out of the ship. Now when he had left speaking, he said unto Simon, Launch out into the deep, and let down your nets for a draught. And Simon answering said unto him, Master, we have toiled all the night, and have taken nothing: nevertheless at thy word I will let down the net. And when they had done this, they inclosed a great multitude of fishes: and their net brake. And they beckoned unto their partners, which were in the other ship, that they should come and help them. And they came, and filled both the ships, so that they began to sink. When Simon Peter saw it, he fell down at Jesus' knees, saying, Depart from me; for I am a sinful man, O Lord. For he was astonished, and all that were with him, at the draught of the fishes which they had taken: And so was also James, and John, the sons of Zebedee, which were partners with Simon. And Jesus said unto Simon, Fear not; from henceforth thou shalt catch men. And when they had brought their ships to land, they forsook all, and followed him.

What we have just read about is the story of Simon Peter's catch of fish. A soldier might have said it was when Peter received his commission. And it really was about the fisherman Simon's call to become a disciple.

What was it that made this man worthy of such a high position? There have been given many explanations for this. And every interpreter has found those characteristics that he considers to be the most important, and, with the help of some clever and sometimes some tricky, manipulation, been able to assign them to Simon, and thereby say: here we have the reasons that this man could be appointed to be the leader of our Lord's disciples.

I believe that the case was this; Jesus chose Simon because of his weakness. He did not have great leadership qualities, this fisherman from Bethsaida. Perhaps he could be stubborn, but could he also be patient? The determined perseverance, the disdain for compromise, and the unfailing confidence that others could rely on—we find nothing of that in him, less than nothing.

Kipling wrote a proud verse about how you should stand by a man once you have committed yourself to him. Simon did not indulge in that type of shining heroism. On the contrary, he was the type that would fail when he was most needed. When it came down to it, when the situation would reveal whether or not he had what it takes to do that for which he was called upon, then he would prove to be a bungler. He has become known the world over as a denier of God. He really isn't worthy stuff for a sermon, not for youth, and even less about Christ. All that which is called idealism hangs with limp wings when it gets close to the son of John. He was right, he was really right, when he said of himself: I am a sinful man. A sinful man, that is what Simon Peter was, and not much more. It says clearly in the stories in the gospel that Jesus was a good judge of character. So it wasn't because of a misjudgment that it was precisely Peter that Jesus chose. Jesus could see through him right from the beginning. He had seen that here was a man with these many faults. But, as He was Jesus, he added: therefore we can use him.

For God is one who rejoices more over a sinner who repents, than over the ninety-nine innocent who have no need to repent. There is more to these words of Jesus than just a cutting irony.

So Peter was then enrolled in the theological seminary at Gennesaret. Today we read about the matriculation ceremony. His certificate of admission was this; he was no good at fishing. *We have fished all night, Master, and caught nothing. So we probably won't catch anything now either. But I am a polite man, and would not want to offend anyone.*

In the course of studies that Peter would be following, Jesus, with his divine knowledge of men, would play a prominent role. But He did not give Peter a new nature. He was, and would remain, the same man. Throughout his life, until his last breath, he was an uncertain soul. But even if Jesus was not able to improve upon him, he was at least able to use him. The great Master was able to use Peter to establish that world kingdom, which is the only one that can really carry His name.

Let's look at a few details. It's been said that it was very nice of Peter that, even though he doubted that it would be of any help, he still acted on the words of Jesus. That was the least that he could do. How could he do otherwise? If he had said no, there would have been an open rift between them, a break for life between the two men. The man that we would have expected to be Jesus' right hand man would have gladly jumped back into the boat, saying *Thanks a lot, Lord!* Wasn't it his Master who spoke? Couldn't he see in the Master's eyes that great things would happen? No, there is nothing inspirational in the sight of this grumbling and unwilling man, this not only doubting, but also directly faithless disciple.

And then Jesus gave him a hold full of fish. He countered one bad habit with generosity. It is Jesus' humorous lesson, a powerful proof of what a great humorist the Saviour is. He doesn't hesitate to *say it with fish*. And the effect is much greater than if he had spoken with fire and brimstone, or struck his insolent disciple with apoplexy. *A curse upon him and all of his followers*, it has been said. *Go away from me, Master, for I am a sinful man*. But again, this strange Master whom he kneels before, laughs. Yes, my friend Simon, now you have proven that you are no good at fishing, and therefore I will make you a greater fisherman. You will start my Fishery of men, the greatest of its kind on earth.

Is it any wonder that they beached their ships, and left everything behind to follow Him?

Peter was quick to words and action. And it often backfired. Why was Jesus was so gentle with him? In his life's deepest fall, Jesus only gave him a glance. He must have known, that for that type of impulsive nature, there is not far between the light blue of heaven and the black depths of despair. But that was not where Jesus needed him. Only once did Jesus really scold him. Otherwise He had his own subtle way with the disciple. There were few who could be trusted less with the keys than Peter. It wasn't because he was unfaithful: but what might he do with them, if he was either too euphoric, or too depressed. Well then, the Saviour *entrusted* him with the keys, the keys to heaven no less. And it has never been said that Peter had misused them. It was first his heirs, who had received them by default, who have sometimes given us reason to complain.

Priceless, and perhaps with the deepest insight, the Master set things in place that day He gave him his new name. He could have called him *The wind*, or *The wave*, and imagined pretty images about the new name. But he called him *The Rock*. Have you heard anything like it? *Simon the Rock!*

Yes, that is what Jesus called him, and what affect it had for the next thirty to forty years of his life! Every time he was about to give up on himself as a hopeless and spineless character, he remembered that the Lord, who knew him, had called him the Rock. And he stood up again, and continued on, with faith in the deepest meaning of the Master's words.

The living stone, he called himself when he was older, in a touching and rather awkward way of imitating his Master's wise humor. Yes, he became the living cornerstone for the Church that would look so much like him: those who would accept Jesus, and love Him, and yet at decisive times deny Him, though they would continue in His congregation, by *His* grace, according to *His* call, and sanctified by it alone.

It seems so significant to me, that among all of the great minds, and honorable, strong characters, as well as the authoritative Pharisees, that there were none of them that found a place among Jesus' followers. None of those who were as strong as a rock were called a rock. It would be he, who was quite the opposite of a rock. Nor do I have anything to offer other than my simple confession: Go away from me, for I am a sinful man. And does He go away? The story about the calling of Simon Peter tells me that I do not believe He did. And that story helps me as well to find strength against despair.

And what of my native land? It is a Christian country, called upon by the Creator Himself to carry His Son's name. They are a clever people, and are in many ways honorable, industrious, and alert. But with respect to the basic question of life, it might have proven to be, in the heat of the decisive moment, a denier. Does that mean it was rejected? Not by the Master who did not reject the disciple who failed Him. He still has His plans for us. His call to Denmark is still in force.

But there is one thing we must not forget when we talk about Peter—and let us remember this, there is one virtue that he did have—*Go away from me, for I am a sinful man.* Or at another time—*then he went outside and wept bitterly.*

The Lord built upon this virtue, as well as upon all his faults, when He gave His disciple the greatest name of all.

Let us remember that, my fellow Christians.

Let us remember that, my countrymen.

20 July 1941
6th Sunday after Trinity
Matthew 5:20-26

The Wrath of God

For I say unto you, that except your righteousness shall exceed the righteousness of the scribes and Pharisees, ye shall in no case enter into the kingdom of heaven.

Ye have heard that it was said by them of old time, Thou shalt not kill; and whosoever shall kill shall be in danger of the judgment: but I say unto you, that whosoever is angry with his brother without a cause shall be in danger of the judgment: and whosoever shall say to his brother, Raca, shall be in danger of the council: but whosoever shall say, Thou fool, shall be in danger of hell fire. Therefore if thou bring thy gift to the altar, and there rememberest that thy brother hath ought against thee; leave there thy gift before the altar, and go thy way; first be reconciled to thy brother, and then come and offer thy gift. Agree with thine adversary quickly, whiles thou art in the way with him; lest at any time the adversary deliver thee to the judge, and the judge deliver thee to the officer, and thou be cast into prison. Verily I say unto thee, Thou shalt by no means come out thence, till thou hast paid the uttermost farthing.

If only it could be done by leaning one's head over, speaking languishingly, or giving gentle and pious handshakes. Yes, then it would be so easy! But our Lord doesn't care at all about such pious pretences. He doesn't look at the labels. He knows! Only the real thing is good enough for Him.

There are many who believe that someone who shouts and screams cannot be a true Christian. If you just say, *damn*, you're condemned. Even among the worst of sinners can be found an image of Christianity that is all too prudish. A Christian, they think, is someone who is nice and modest, timid and cautious; he cannot allow himself to do that, which we others, who have no such pretences, find natural.

The clergy itself has been so cowardly that it has even sided with the boasters. It has been afraid to challenge its opponents, or to offend the pious old women. We know the *Dear Friend* sermons, we know the *Dear you*, greetings, and we know the always-gracious smiles.

That is the phony righteousness of the scholars and the Pharisees. It has sent the church not into heaven, nor into hell, but into complete irrelevance. And that is a lie. Christ has never demanded that man deny his nature.

Then what has He demanded? Hasn't He taught us that God is love! Doesn't He still teach us that we shall love each other?

But what is love? Is it just another word for honey cake? No, love is passion. It doesn't need to show off. It sees eunuchs as an abomination. And when Christ has been able, throughout many centuries, to inspire youth to take up His cause, to imbue proud men with the humility for martyrdom, and weak women with the resolve to sacrifice throughout their lives, then it is because He Himself has felt that passion, and at that a passion for the greatest thing: love.

For the greatest passion is love, that which wants only to give eternal joy to another.

And for Jesus, therefore, God was the God of wrath, in whom there was nothing weak or sweet. That man might be transformed to possess His spirit, so that instead of being angry at each other, and harassing each other, they would find brothership together. This is so important to Him, that all means will be used to make it happen. This is not just an interesting idea that has been put forth, nor an original philosophy that has been proposed; it is serious—it is God's sincerity. And those who defy this sincerity will feel the wrath of God.

Yes, but we cannot just love each other. How can the staff of a school not be angry with the principal when he offends? How can Mrs. Hansen avoid being jealous when Mrs. Jensen has gotten a new hat? How can the parish pastor put up with the curate when the customers flock to his sale of the gospel at reduced prices? And the political parties—and the colliding races—How can mankind exist without hatred?

And to speak of the Saviour Himself! How could it be that He could entertain those men who were His competitors for the hearts of the people? He apparently did not simply give in to his adversaries. Vipers and zombies were two names he gave them. And yet, toward the unsuspecting but respectable businessmen in the temple, he acted like a thug.

But this was all a part of his burning passion. Aflame in His wrath of love, He struck out against the menace of evil. Holy in His zeal for love, He struck out without pity against the spirit that would cast mankind into the clutches of hate.

But when it concerned Himself, and not His cause, then He was as a lamb is to the one who shears it. Then he healed the ear of the high priest's servant, he embraced the denier with His forgiving glance, and then He said that prayer, which became the world's most unforgettable: *Forgive them, Father, for they know not what they do.*

What He has preached to us, He has also shown to us, and He has lived it for us, to the last bitter dregs. Well, He is God's Son, the church teacher says, but we are not conceived outside of nature, we are in the clutches of the flesh, and must follow our instincts. It is necessary, in this hard world, to defend oneself, and fight fire with fire, so that the others behave.

Well, perhaps they will. But we are again approaching an age that, even more clearly than earlier, reminds us that the continued technological development brings with it the principles of an eye for an eye, and tooth for a tooth. And that can result in the destruction of mankind by its own hand.

Well, but what if the other principle, that of Jesus, is by nature, impossible?

Again the church prefers pleasantries, rather than love. It has a sermon at the ready. It tells us about an ideal, it reminds us of our own impotence, about the Redeemer atoning for our sins, about God's eternal mercy. It is a pretty sermon, and very profound.

But today's text doesn't talk at all about that. It says in plain language, that the Word of God requires of man that he show brotherly love to his fellow man; and if he doesn't, then he will feel the wrath of God.

There is no reason to preach more about that. It is an idea that speaks for itself.

These are not easy words. They are so intractable. Not really very Christian. But whether it is Christian or not, they are the words of Jesus. Jesus can sometimes be so terribly straightforward—not profound, brilliant, or symbolic—but simply true.

But I can prove, through the use of science and other undeniable disciplines, that if I am by nature prone to survival, then I cannot destroy myself. You might be able to demand of the lion that it eat grass, but....

And Jesus hears our objections and excuses, but repeats: *Verily I say unto thee, Thou shalt by no means come out thence, till thou hast paid the last farthing.*

So strict is the Lord of love. If the words He speaks mean anything at all to us, then they will send shivers down our backs—the teachers, Mrs. Jensen, the pastor, and everyone else. We would rather go to church and hear some warm and fervent sermon about sin; with such bottomless depth that only God's mercy can reach that deep. But Christ is unpleasant enough to say to us: *What in the world do you go to church for? You can wait with that until you have made peace with your brother.*

Do you hear that, young people, do you hear that proud and passionate voice calling you away from nonsense and affectation, from indifference and defeat, from all that witchcraft that the world would paralyze you with. That voice is calling you to fight against the world's spirit and against your own nature. Not for something unnatural, but for something supernatural, for the struggle for the kingdom of love in a world of hatred—the most impossible of all, and therefore the greatest of all. It calls you away from the curse of denial, away from showy hypocrisy and foolishness, and toward *esse non videri (To be, not to seem)*, to really be that which alone can endure.

And you, my listeners: each one of you, who has been painfully touched, because you have an unsettled dispute with someone—I threaten you with God's wrath—if you do not go home at once and try to straighten it out, you will be haunted on your death bed if you flout the words of God that you have heard today.

27 July 1941
7th Sunday after Trinity
Mark 8:1-9

Faith in the Invisible

In those days the multitude being very great, and having nothing to eat, Jesus called his disciples unto Him, and saith unto them, I have compassion on the multitude, because they have now been with me three days, and have nothing to eat: And if I send them away fasting to their own houses, they will faint by the way: for divers of them came from far. And his disciples answered him, From whence can a man satisfy these men with bread here in the wilderness? And he asked them, How many loaves have ye? And they said, Seven. And he commanded the people to sit down on the ground: and he took the seven loaves, and gave thanks, and brake, and gave to his disciples to set before them; and they did set them before the people. And they had a few small fishes: and He blessed, and commanded to set them also before them. So they did eat, and were filled: and they took up the broken meat that was left seven baskets. And they that had eaten were about four thousand: and he sent them away.

The Lord Jesus is a brave man. How did He dare to perform this miracle? What can be more dangerous than giving food to people who have not done a thing to earn it? What can be more risky for a man who wants to win the hearts of the people than to show them he has power?

There is nothing that proves man's depravity more than his behavior toward power. Not even his passions and carnal desires reveal his sickening vulgarity more.

Power threatens, and then cowardice steps aside. Power entices, and then lust comes wagging its tail. And as far as idealism goes—nothing is easier for Power to overcome than idealism. Idealism doesn't have time to ask if what is happening is right. No, it probably is, but it is enough that it's great—even if all divine and human laws get trampled on, that doesn't matter, as long as something great is happening. Power doesn't argue, it just points at its results, and see; young eyes shine, and warm hearts beat in time.

But our Lord knew all about that. He lived in a land where He could see it every day. He knew how power used that gimmick called *results*.

It was for that reason that He was so careful not to appear successful. How often we hear about Him, that when He had performed a miracle he would ask those who had been there to be silent about what they had seen, because He did not believe in power, not at all. He was never overwhelmed when He heard the tramping of feet in the road, the thought that the same tramping was heard from the North Sea to the Euphrates. He didn't think about it. He probably wasn't even aware of it.

For He had the unshakeable faith that none of that meant anything. It was like a play with soap bubbles and foam.

This was the truth about the *results*; the visible, the concrete, and the great.

Power sows its dragon teeth across the world. It crows over what it has accomplished, for everyone can see that it is winning. But what a fool! For hate grows so relentlessly in the gloomy world of the suppressed? And one day it will take its best shot, and overthrow that which calls itself the eternal state. What can power create other than weakness, first that of others, and later its own?

Christ never said a bad word about the Romans. Why should he have? There were so many others willing to do that. He hardly knew they existed, and paid little attention to them. He had greater things to think about.

He turned his eyes toward the invisible. *Yours is the power for eternity,* He said. He planted His faith in the invisible in the midst of the visible world, and that faith grew steadily, and blew the Roman Empire to pieces.

It was said that it was mostly slaves and freedmen that joined this new movement, and everyone could see that they had no power. But it was these, the powerless, that vanquished power.

But today, my listeners, He lets us see into the secret world, which is the real world. Against all rules He lets mankind glimpse the invisible. The seven loaves and a few small fish are nothing—but laid in His hands, lifted up to heaven, and blessed by the hidden up there, He, whose spirit is love—they can feed four thousand hungry men in the desert.

Why did He do it? Didn't He know how dangerous it was? That they would think it was about food? That they would make Him king so that He could go on to perform miracles? That He was about to betray the principle of faith: to see is just confusing—it is with faith, and only faith, that the world can be conquered.

And these were not just trivial objections. There really were some of His disciples who later turned against Him, disappointed in their expectations that He wanted a kingdom in this world. Could He really deny that He was partly to blame for these expectations, after performing such a miracle?

And plan economists might say: *We can't learn anything from that man; He can give people a dinner out of thin air, but that is not an option for us.*

I started to say that Jesus was a brave man. He didn't care about these objections, and instead followed the voice in His heart. He was deeply touched by the hungry, and had the power to help. And so He helped.

If only we all did that!

But He might have had another purpose with it. He had preached long enough, and now they would *see* a sermon that they would never forget. Maybe some would not understand; but there would always be some among them who would never forget this sight of God. Even if they would later see their children starve to death, and follow along the same way, they would never forget Him, His power, and His love, that they saw that afternoon in Galilee. And they would go to their death with faith in this power and this love.

Seven loaves of bread, and a few small fish! I go up to my pulpit and feel that it is so little I have to say about the wealth that fills me, and I go down again from the pulpit, feeling like a traitor—I had betrayed God's glory by standing there, feeble and stuttering. And yet I had the greatest message of all to bear witness to. And I go to other churches, and my colleagues there do no better. And yet, Sunday after Sunday, though we pastors seem such stale fish, our Lord's blessings reach out, through us, to thousands upon thousands.

And the sacraments—baptism, a sprinkling of water over a baby's head by a civil servant; the Eucharist, a piece of dry bread and a sip of cheap wine—but the mystery of God's grace is hidden in these, for in the smallest thing the greatest of all lies hidden.

And then the Christian church itself—aren't we rather strange? Science and art, politics and the military, sport and finances—we do not pluck these pretty blossoms in our Lord's modest convent garden. They really cannot tolerate us, and we can barely tolerate each other. But, the apostle says, God has chosen the poor and despised of the world, and that agrees as well with the Lord's accounting. That, which seems not to be, is manifest—for we are the salt of the earth, we are the light of the world, and we have inherited eternity.

This little unlikely sunshine story about the few loaves and small fish in the desert, enough for 4,000 men—there is power in that! Power that can make us smile at the illusion of grandeur that can make others stand gaping on shaky legs, power that helps us to see the invisible, and even in the midst of a world of crass materialism, to believe in the insignificant, the scorned, the almighty—that which is called Spirit.

10 August 1941
9th Sunday after Trinity
Luke 16:1-9

The Unfaithful Steward

And he said also unto his disciples, There was a certain rich man, which had a steward; and the same was accused unto him that he had wasted his goods. And he called him, and said unto him, How is it that I hear this of thee? give an account of thy stewardship; for thou mayest be no longer steward. Then the steward said within himself, What shall I do? for my lord taketh away from me the stewardship: I cannot dig; to beg I am ashamed. I am resolved what to do, that, when I am put out of the stewardship, they may receive me into their houses. So he called every one of his lord's debtors unto him, and said unto the first, How much owest thou unto my lord? And he said, An hundred measures of oil. And he said unto him, Take thy bill, and sit down quickly, and write fifty. Then said he to another, And how much owest thou? And he said, An hundred measures of wheat. And he said unto him, Take thy bill, and write fourscore. And the lord commended the unjust steward, because he had done wisely: for the children of this world are in their generation wiser than the children of light. And I say unto you, Make to yourselves friends of the mammon of unrighteousness; that, when ye fail, they may receive you into everlasting habitations.

The unfaithful steward is not a title that we would want to have on our gravestone. But rather the opposite. If there is one thing we fervently pray to God for, it is that we may be judged faithful. There are words of Christ that are as beautiful as a fata morgana, and they are the words about faith. He has told us that there will be those on judgment day who He will greet with: *...well done, good and faithful servant; thou hast been faithful* *over a few things, I will make thee ruler over many things: enter thou into the joy of thy Lord.* Every Christian thinks that this is an impossibility, that such a judgment could actually be upon them on that great day, and yet every Christian prays that it may somehow happen.

And, especially in these times, it is our heartfelt prayer that we may be faithful. And that is because right now it is so difficult to be faithful, and because there is now so much at stake. There is a Danish leader who coined a proud word about not compromising with injustice. Christian Berg[7] is dead, but injustice is still alive.

Well, one could almost smile at what they used to call injustice. The struggles of that time are beginning to look pretty idyllic. And yet it was the same struggle. Wisdom and cowardice have always supported each other in the belief that compromise is the best solution. Those who are driven by faith in their hearts do not believe in such wisdom, and despise such cowardice.

There is a deep connection between belief and faithfulness, between believing and being faithful. And it is for that reason that people, who have no beliefs, but only standpoints, have no trouble going from one to another. They will defend a position today just as strongly as they defended the opposite position yesterday. And they have no inclination to regret their changing positions. Rather they feel that they are doing the right thing. And they are apparently right about that. They have, after all, not betrayed anything. They are not even capable of doing that. As Nis Petersen[8] says, they can comfortably cash in on any momentary victory.

But faith does not count on the momentary victory—it counts on *sacrifice and sober resolve*. It is a heavy burden that does not encourage flip-flops. It counts the stars, while the others count the money.

And yet faith does—implausibly but true—believe that it *can* pay off. It rejects completely the idea that betrayal and cheating can lead to anything of value. Faith is based on the belief that real value lies in that which first brings loss—in honor, self-denial, and sacrifice. Faith knows that even if deceit appears to ascend toward heaven, its victory procession will surely end in hell.

But at the same time faith knows, that even if it were mistaken, so that it becomes the loser for all time, it still would not trade. For no matter what honor, self-denial, or sacrifice bring about in this life, or the next, it is, and will be, that which is most noble.

Probably the greatest difference between the children of Adam is this: there are those who swear to what is noble, and then there are those who swear to what is profitable.

We Christians in Denmark pray to God to preserve us in our faith. Faith in what we love—our country and our Christianity—the two kingdoms that we have been born and baptized into, and in the faith that gives us strength, so that with heroic conviction and a martyr's courage, we will still believe, no matter how many of us may deceive and cheat. And we pray to God to grant us the vision of the Holy Spirit, so that we can see through the clever arguments of deceit, no matter how many of those who we trusted and felt close to, are tricked and confused by them.

Yes, God, grant that we will love faithfulness above all else.

But what is this for a sermon about the unfaithful steward? Haven't we learned in today's text that Christ holds up the unfaithful steward as an example for us?

The unfaithful steward, that is the Lord's parable that has most vexed the poor interpreters. In the sweat of their brows they have toiled and struggled with this text so that it could be turned into a decent sermon, fit for the pulpit.

And yet this story is very straightforward. And it is tremendously courageous. It says to all God fearing people: *you have a lot to learn from the devil!*

And that is the brutal truth.

I think it might have gone like this: Jesus read an article in the Capernaum Times about the latest case of fraud. And then He again wondered about how the children of this world are so self-centered, in comparison to the children of light.

The loathsome character in this story, who lives well by cheating his Master, and who eventually can do little else but cheat—this fine man, who is too good to beg, but not too good to commit forgery—you have to admire him! Some day justice will prevail, but he will not give up for that reason. He will not be tying any nooses. Rather, he will mobilize his cunning for one last decisive stand. *So, my friend, it's a hundred measures of oil you owe? We can soon expect a visit by the Master, but I know about your financial problems. I don't see anything wrong in just erasing that, and writing fifty instead.*

He's a nice guy, this steward! He has a heart for the little man! A really nice guy!

Then the master arrives, expecting to find an exposed wretch begging in panic. But the steward is quite calm. If master is not satisfied with his service, well, he can just leave.

He has saved himself in the nick of time, and is out of danger. The master has to conceal a smile when he sees through him. What a crook!

But it's a different story when once again a day of reckoning comes for the unfaithful steward. In all his preparations, he had forgotten to plan for that. But the master who will interrogate him this time does not conceal a smile.

But, as it's been said, that is another story, as Jesus has so often told us. But what the Saviour was thinking about here is quite simply this:

You should be ashamed of yourselves, you, who are my disciples. You fight for the eternal goal, and yet are half-hearted, spineless, and complacent. But those who fight for themselves, for the treasures of this world, for the *values* that wilt and rot as soon as they get them, see what they can muster of passion, thought, and imagination!

Yes, this is the bitter truth. We again get a taste of the whip. Let us read world history, and see what sacrifices have been made for purely secular goals. But what fires have been lit to inspire the young, and with what fervor has the love of pleasure been suppressed? All that we should have been doing ourselves, the others have done instead.

It's high time that the Christian church obeys the words of Jesus, and learns as well from these others. God Himself is not afraid to use the devil in His service. He often uses scoundrels to punish scoundrels.

The history of the people of Israel abounds with examples of this. We, who are His children, must not be afraid to learn from His examples, or from our enemies. The ingenuity and endurance that the unfaithful steward uses to reach his goal, is what we must use to reach ours. The ferocity with which he fights against evil must make us give up the defense of the good, and instead go on the attack for it. The ruthlessness with which he is faithless, should inflame our passion to keep our faith.

7 September 1941
13th Sunday after Trinity
Luke 10:23-37

The Good Samaritan

And He turned Him unto His disciples, and said privately, Blessed are the eyes which see the things that ye see: for I tell you, that many prophets and kings have desired to see those things which ye see, and have not seen them; and to hear those things which ye hear, and have not heard them.

And behold, a certain lawyer stood up, and tempted him, saying, Master, what shall I do to inherit eternal life? He said unto him, What is written in the law? how readest thou? And he answering said, Thou shalt love the Lord thy God with all thy heart, and with all thy soul, and with all thy strength, and with all thy mind; and thy neighbour as thyself. And he said unto him, Thou hast answered right: this do, and thou shalt live. But he, willing to justify himself, said unto Jesus, And who is my neighbour? And Jesus answering said, A certain man went down from Jerusalem to Jericho, and fell among thieves, which stripped him of his raiment, and wounded him, and departed, leaving him half dead. And by chance there came down a certain priest that way: and when he saw him, he passed by on the other side. And likewise a Levite, when he was at the place, came and looked on him, and passed by on the other side. But a certain Samaritan, as he journeyed, came where he was: and when he saw him, he had compassion on him, and went to him, and bound up his wounds, pouring in oil and wine, and set him on his own beast, and brought him to an inn, and took care of him. And on the morrow when he departed, he took out two pence, and gave them to the host, and said unto him, Take care of him; and whatsoever thou spendest more, when I come again, I will repay thee. Which now of these three, thinkest thou, was neighbour unto him that fell among the thieves? And he said, He that shewed mercy on him. Then said Jesus unto him, Go, and do thou likewise.

Blessed are the eyes that see the things that ye see—those are Jesus' words to us. Yes, to us. Not just to Peter and John, and the others of that time. But to all of us, who in one way or another have found Jesus, and have learned his secret—that he is God's living Son.

I look back at my own eyes, and ask them: *Are you two happy now?* And they look back at me, disgruntled, and answer: *not even close!*

And why not, I ask impatiently? And they answer by showing me the things that they see everyday—the sight of horror, of sorrow, of the works of the devil, of triumph and oppression in the wide world—and here at home in our little world, the precious one we call Denmark, a lack of sorrow, a sense of self satisfaction: *Haven't we done pretty well?* And they see death, scandal, and decay.

But listen here you two eyes; nobody has said that you have to be so happy about filling yourselves with the events of the world. Are you forgetting, in the midst of all that which overwhelms you every day, to turn towards that image which alone can give you happiness, the image of Him, our Saviour?

You, thou great Holy Spirit, it is my eyes' sorrow that they look downward too much, and upward too little. Teach them to share their attention evenly between down and up; but not to look so much upward that life here becomes irrelevant for them, and they get by just looking after their own satisfaction through the ecstasy of bliss. Nor too much downward, so that they are tortured and bewildered, and end up distraught and empty. O Holy Spirit, dry the tears from my eyes, so that I might see the Saviour, see Him clearly enough to tell my people about Him, now in their fateful hour.

That is how we Danish pastors pray in 1941. The pulpit has become our place of reckoning, so we tremble in our black vestments as we ascend the stairs. For here, in God's house, the Word is set free—but not in the sense that we can decide what to say, but in the sense that the Word prevails over us. In here the only censor is the Holy Spirit, and that forces us not to be silent, but to speak. And so it is out of fear when we are not faithful servants, and it is an obligation upon us that the new has come! Before it was the individual that we aimed at, the congregation, and it still is. And for the sake of life and death and eternity, it is important that that work is not set aside. But now we understand, even better than before, that God is also Denmark's God, and that Jesus is not just the individual's Saviour, he is also our people's Saviour. And maybe the church is not involved in economic planning, or the New Europe, or national ideology, but it is the place where injustice shall be exiled, lies shall be exposed, and poison brought to light—the place where mercy shall be nourished as the source of life, as the heart of man—and where we learn not just of the faith, but also of the jungle and of death.

There is an ancient interpretation of *The Good Samaritan*. It tells us that it is mankind itself that lies in the ditch along the Jericho-Jerusalem road, severely battered by the wild horde of hatred and lust. There are of course some supermen who cannot accept that comparison, the movers and shakers who refuse to be labelled as wretches in the ditch. Their faces—hard, lustful, or cruel—clearly reveal the powers that have occupied their souls.

The interpretations of the Lord's parables go further: The Good Samaritan is Jesus Himself; He has bowed down over the fallen world and lifted it up. He has told it about God's endless mercy. He has saved our lives; and now we are on the road to redemption.

That is a beautiful Christian interpretation. It says what Jesus had so often told us, actually what He had told us with His life. But this interpretation of the parable is not correct. It is like bringing owls to Athens, and that might not hurt anything, except that Athens has its own owls!

And that is the case here. Christianity is an ellipse about two centers. One of them says: Man is powerless, and depends on God for everything. And the other says: Man is powerful; he decides his own fate; and, he is so powerful that he can defy God.

That other truth, the possibility of man's free will, is what the parable throws in our face. The self-important legal mind was taught that *neighbour* is not a legal or theoretical a concept. *Neighbour* is a person of flesh and bone. His name is Rasmus Hansen; her name is Kirstine Pedersen. It is your servant, your cook, your train conductor, and your king. Your neighbour is everyone you are involved with. And you always have this choice: you can either be good to your fellow man, or you can be a burden. There are some who you can help by saving them from thieves. And there are others you can help by killing them. Literally. Niels Ebbesen versus Count Gert[9], for example. The bald count would have earned many more years in hell, if his crimes had not been stopped on 1 April 1340.

And if it wasn't out of consideration for the count, then it was at least an act of mercy toward the downtrodden and suffering people.

Blessed are the eyes which see the things that ye see, the Saviour said to His believers. Yes, we are blessed because we see Him. He is our source of light and life. He has shared with us the eternal joy by letting God's love shine upon us. Every time we see that the world is evil, he lifts our eyes so that we can see that God is good. Not a sentimental and silly goodness. "Love your enemy" doesn't mean that you have to give in to him, and agree with him. No, you should love him so much that you would rather spit in his face than commit the crime of letting him believe that you will be silent and agree with his enterprise and methods. You should love him because he is a fellow man, but you should hate him when he is the perpetrator of evil; if, that is, he is your enemy for the sake of truth, and not just for the sake of yourself. Yes, there are, God help them, people who suffer from a cancerous Christian love; they believe that the Good Samaritan sought out the thieves afterwards, and complimented them for a job well done. God's goodness is such, that it is meek and long-suffering, but never compromises with evil. He lets sin run its course, and then breaks it. And all of those who were its tool; they will be struck by the fury of God's love.

And so it is our prayer to the Holy Spirit that He will fulfil his great work in our hearts in these trying times, and that Jesus may shine bright before us. Then nothing will defeat us, and our eyes will be blessed. With overflowing joy in their hearts, the parishioners will see, and those who seek will learn, from His quiet and proud behaviour, when we should say no, and when we should say yes, and how we should behave and do our work, so that it helps our neighbour and our country.

16 November 1941
23rd Sunday after Trinity
Matthew 22: 15,22

God and Caesar

"Christianity takes orders from nobody."

Then went the Pharisees and took counsel how they might entangle him in his talk. And they sent out unto him their disciples, with the Herodians, saying, Master, we know that thou art true, and teachest the way of God in truth, neither carest thou for any man: for thou regardest not the person of men. Tell us therefore, what thinkest thou? Is it lawful to give tribute unto Caesar, or not? But Jesus perceived their wickedness, and said, Why tempt ye me, ye hypocrites? Show me the tribute-money. And they brought unto him a penny. And he saith unto them, Whose is this image and superscription? They say unto him, Caesar's. Then saith he unto them, Render therefore unto Caesar the things which are Caesar's; and unto God the things that are God's. When they heard these words, they marvelled, and left him, and went their way.

We hear today that the Herodians and the Pharisees have formed a kind of coalition government. There wasn't much they could agree on, except that they both hate Jesus. But see how graciously they come to Him: they must be a cultured people! *Master, we know that thou art true, and teachest the way of God in truth, neither carest thou for any man: for thou regardest not the person of men.*

How beautifully said. We are almost moved to tears!

And anyhow, it's strange how it goes with that type of person. They thought they were lying, and yet it was the pure truth they were speaking. And when they think they are speaking the truth, you can be sure it's a lie.

The way they formulated their questions was an obvious attempt to trap Jesus. They really tried to provoke Him into carelessness. But it would have been easy for Him to avoid that. He could have just said, *Problems with collecting tax for Caesar are not in my department; earthly kingdoms are not within my domain; I am only concerned with heavenly kingdoms.*

The Saviour could easily have answered evasively. And He must have been well aware of the danger in offending the country's most powerful parties.

And now, when He opens his mouth to speak, the first thing that comes out—we are excited; now we will see if He is a Christian or a coward—It's a term of abuse, such a beautiful and straightforward term of abuse.

You hypocrites, He says.

What might have been lost in tone was made up for in clarity. Now the two parties knew where they had each other.

Show me the tribute-money!

He is not a man who hesitates and ponders. His is not a contemptible character. The answer is ready in the same moment the question is asked.

Whose is this image and superscription?

Caesars.

Render therefore unto Caesar the things which are Caesar's; and unto God the things that are God's.

These images of Jesus—it is a strange thing about them—they are images for all time, they are immortal art.

The situation had been settled; there was nothing to add or subtract. But at the same time an answer had been given for all time. No dead rules, but the voice of life. A provocative and inspiring answer! It is the duty of Christians to give to Caesar that which is Caesar's, and we have obeyed that command. We have been the most law-abiding citizens in the nation. But, if Caesar demanded more than his share, then there would be none more rebellious than we. And indomitable we would remain, year after year, decade after decade, and century after century—until we were victorious.

He could demand much of us: our money, our labor, the best years of our youth, our health, and our life.

But if he demanded that we call black white, tyranny freedom, lies truth, conquest and violence justice, then we answered him: it is written—thou shalt have no other Gods before me.

And if he asked that again of us, we would answer: it is written—*thou shall not take the Lord's name in vain.*

Let him come with his lions and tigers, his gallows, and his stakes. The blood of Christians is like seed, they said in the ancient church. We are victorious in death. We must obey God before man.

Render therefore unto Caesar the things which are Caesar's; and unto God the things that are God's. The Christian has a home in both of these great kingdoms. But if they should clash, he knows at once which one is his greatest obligation.

That's all well and good, but Christianity must be non-political, some say. And who decides that? Christianity takes orders from nobody.

Well, all right. Let's say that it is non-political. But is it? Yes, in a way. But that is just as true as it is false.

One can be a conservative, a communist, or anything in between, and at the same time a Christian. That is true enough. Christianity will reveal itself in the manner in which one is a conservative or a communist. But if that is taken to mean that Christianity has simply learned to hold its nose for the things of the world, then it is a mistake.

Let's keep politics out of the church, some say; we hear enough of politics on the radio, and read about it in the newspapers. Let's be free of that in the house of God.

But how is it that we hear about it on the radio, and read about in the papers? Perhaps we should hear about it in God's house, but in a different way than we are used to. In God's house we should hear about what happens in the world, judged in relation to the word of God.

We should also talk about Caesar in church, and about his relationship to God.

There are some who would want us to believe that the church is only a refuge for the soul, and that the church should not get involved with anything other than saving souls.

Yes, that's some nice religion! If little Jensen can just look after himself and get into heaven, why should he care about the world? It can go straight to hell.

Now that's a religion that Caesar would like. He would probably give it a subsidy. Then it would stay out of his way, and never cause him problems. It is the religion called blasphemy.

Well, the church is a sanctuary, some would explain to me; there should be peace and grandeur about a divine service. Is that right? Not if it is achieved through lies and subterfuge. Divine service that is afraid of the truth is the Devil's service. And the truth is not quiet, nor dignified, nor exalted. It bites and scratches and strikes.

The truth is not for cautious people. They would prefer the sofa to the truth.

What is it for a meaningless demand that the church be cautious? Was Christ cautious? Were the martyrs cautious?

Hush, hush, hush! is today's solution. *As otherwise it might have serious consequences for the nation.* That's right. But silence and subterfuge can have even greater consequences.

Then I would prefer Jesus! *You hypocrites, swindlers, and whited sepulchres,* he called the demagogues in his land. *Give my greetings to that fox*, he scornfully called Herod, who had ingratiated himself with the Roman army in Palestine.

It won't get any better in Denmark until the Danish people learn from Christ's courage. (With us it's more likely that the courageous man will be called a criminal, and thrown in prison.)

At the inauguration of parliament this year, the pastor gave a courageous Christian invocation. Were the members of parliament inspired? Well, many of them simply asked: Do you think we'll get through it?

They should have cried, and wrung their hands together in thanks to God that they had finally heard a Christian man speak. But instead they sniffed and tested the air: Do you think we'll get through it?

This nation will not be a nation worthy of life, until it overcomes its fear. It is nearly dying of caution.

The forbidden sermons
#1- May 1943

Christ and John the Baptist

The most dangerous lie of all is the truth not told

John the Baptist was not a cautious man. He believed in the truth.

King Herod was an adulterer. John went to him, and told him to stop.

He risked his life by doing that. And he risked more than that. He risked causing a rebellion and a civil war. Yes, it could have gone so far that the Romans would have used it as a pretext to intervene, and that would have been a bloody story for the Jewish people.

Why didn't John keep quiet? That would have been a lot wiser, and much more thoughtful.

But would it have?

John was consumed by a burning belief—the belief that the truth is there to be told.

Some people believe that the truth can be pickled. That it can be put up in a jar, kept in brine, and brought out when a bit is needed.

They are mistaken. The truth cannot be pickled. It can only exist as a living thing. And it must be used the moment it appears. If it's not used, it will die and rot, and then decay. The most dangerous lie of all is the truth not told.

John the Baptist was a man of flesh and blood. Flesh is a body with nerves, and blood should stay in the body where it is meant to circulate. The disciples, who were so fond of John, advised him to be careful, and they weren't the only ones. His own flesh and blood warned him: *Herod is a powerful man now. This is not the time to antagonize him; wait until his favour with the people is in decline, or he in some clumsy way loses favour with the Romans. The truth does not suffer from being saved; it will still be the truth. And when the time comes you can step forward with your prophetic might, and knock down the crumbling building.*

But John was not simply a man of flesh and blood. He was also a man of spirit—of God's Spirit, and the spirit of truth. And therefore he did not believe at all in the notion that truth could be pickled.

The day came when he felt the time for action had come. *The truth has come to me, and now it demands to be brought into the light.* His heart beat wildly in his chest, and his tongue was quiet. But within this beating heart there was a great peace: *Now I am speaking as I should speak, now I am answering my call, now I am acting as a man should act.* Yes, in his uneasy heart there was a great peace. It gave his tongue the strength to speak, and to say to Herod the few, but necessary, words: *It is not lawful for thee to have her.*

Peace be with you is the church's greeting. Our hymnal sings of God's Peace, which is more than just the guardian angel singing. And every Sunday we pastors lift up our hands before the altar, and spread them out across the congregation: *The Lord lift up His countenance upon thee, and give thee peace.* It is a terrible mistake to think that this *peace* means hello or good-bye, live well, sleep well, have a good one, or that God will make sure you have a pair of boots for snowy weather. No, God's peace means that your soul is at peace, because no matter how uneasy it may be, it has found peace in its relation to the truth. Peace is a difficult word. The truth is always on the march. So here, peace means to march together with the truth.

It was this peace that was John's guardian angel when he stood before Herod; it couldn't protect his body, but it gave him stature and dignity for all time. It brought contentment to his mind: God's will shall now be done.

The Bible tells about those times in such a way that it applies even today. The story about John the Baptist took place in a distant land in antiquity. But this is happening here in Denmark in 1942.

There are among us good men who have a burning belief in the truth, that it must be told—and that it is only there when it is told. They do not believe that the truth can be put up and stored away. And they cannot go around as if nothing has happened, and let the truth lie in an open grave. They are of flesh and blood, like John, and they too fear for their own fate. And they feel the fear of the devastation that the truth can inflict upon their people. But the day has come when they know that cowardice can no longer silence their tongues, and that the devastation that hypocrisy, silence, and lies inflicts upon their people will, in the long run, prove to be a thousand times worse fate.

And so the great peace will fill their hearts, as it filled John's, when they go to the Herod of our native land, and charge him with adultery.

For even in our country there is a Herod who lies with foreign goddesses, a compromiser, who for the sake of creature comforts, wallows in disgrace.

Herod, of course, had many excuses for breaking the law. He was in love with this woman, you see, and it is right for a man to be moved by great emotions. This relationship granted him the strength for his royal service, and therefore benefited the entire kingdom. Yes, it was only for the sake of the people that he broke the law, and they were satisfied with that, and everything was fine for a while, better than one would have expected in those uneasy times with the enemy occupying the country. Yes, there was actually a lot to be thankful for.

And then this ox from the desert comes along, with something so petty as the truth. He'll butt his head against the wall, and try to topple the edifice that Herod had so carefully erected and maintained until now.

It is worth noting that John the Baptist doesn't get into a dialogue with this slimy serpent. He simply says to him: *It is not lawful for thee to have her.*

John wielded the axe of righteousness. Herod was just a little branch on the tree of injustice. But big or little, judgment had fallen upon him. This *branch*[10] must be cut away.

Nor did his majesty the king enter into discussions. He sent a messenger for the handcuffs. And it has always been that way. The truth has the word on its side, and the lie has swords and chains. But the lie also lies to itself, and will therefore strive to believe that it is the mightiest.

And then John was imprisoned. He had said what he had to say; the darkness of the cell closed around him, and he could feel the sword of death over his head. But God's peace filled his heart—the approval of a good conscience.

What kind of a sinister book is the Bible? Is it telling us now that a good conscience isn't enough, and that even God's peace can vanish from our heart?

Couldn't the Bible have glossed over these very brutal facts? This business about John losing faith while in prison—couldn't it in some more reverent way simply have hurried on to the end, and just have let John fall without a blemish, and sound like a fighter and martyr for the greatest cause of all: the struggle of faith against lawlessness, lies, and tyranny? Alas, the Bible is a primitive book, and is no good at diplomacy, or the culture of propaganda. We have to take the Bible as it is. There is nothing to be done about it. It too is inspired by this crude and dangerous faith in the truth. It tells us that John did begin to doubt, and that it is good for us to know that.

He was alone in his cell. There was no one to hear him, to be inspired by him, or to strengthen his faith by being moved to anger by his words. There was nobody. It was as if he had been forgotten, and nothing happened. Herod was not reproached for his adulterous life. And the people revealed their cowardice, accepting that their favorite prophet languished in prison as the reward for his faithfulness. They wanted to cheer for the truth, as long as it was free. But when the cheering was given a price tag, they became discretely quiet, and let John make the payments. Why had He made this great sacrifice when nothing came of it? Was the truth even true, when it did nothing, and performed no miracles? He, whom John had believed was The Truth, and who he had pledged his life to, was He really the Promised One? *And John calling unto him two of his disciples sent them to Jesus, saying, Art thou He that should come? or look we for another?*

I honestly admit that I don't understand why Jesus did not visit his friend from youth in prison, and that he did nothing to intervene. But I do not feel authorised to criticise Christ. Jesus must have known that there was something that John had to endure on his own. Is it part of the nature of truth that it at times requires that a man must be very much alone?

And yet I am so happy over the words that Jesus spoke to the multitude about the imprisoned and fallen prophet. And it was a hard rebuke that John, who had started Jesus on his mission, and had given himself as a foundation to build upon, would now, publicly, throw such a question in His face. Jesus had reason to be shaken and painfully moved. And the multitudes were clearly ready to drop their old hero for the new man of the hour. Hear how they talked about him: *We wouldn't have believed it about John. What a weakling! As unreliable as a wave or a passing breeze! His religion was probably not worth much, since it couldn't stand the test when it mattered most.*

Yes, those who risk nothing are always critical when those who do risk something do not endure!

See how bravely and resoundingly Christ defends His friend. He is not one who judges people by their heroics. No, He throws Himself into John's defence with all of his untested authority: *Because he is weakened now, you shall not forget what he was, and what he sacrificed at the height of his powers. Then he did not bend like a reed in the wind, nor plant a foot in each camp. Go to the parliament if you want to see that type of person! John should not be judged by what he was, or what he became, but by what he did when it mattered most, when he fulfilled his life's destiny. That will give him eternal fame. That, and nothing else but that, was John. That moment was his life's destiny; in that deed he was the torchbearer of the truth—a messenger from God.*

Jesus is magnanimous towards those who fail—as long as they wanted to do the right thing at the right time. *I ask, Lord Jesus, that you grant me your great spirit! Should I have a friend, who once sang the words of truth for my people, but has since failed miserably—help me, Lord Jesus. Give me the courage to refrain from anger and contempt. Give me, despite what he is now, the strength to honor his name for what he was.*

Look, Salome is dancing in the castle. They are having a great time there. It's a New Year's party, and the entire castle has been made up like a *Night on the Wild Side*. And this man, who has been appointed the servant of justice, and guardian of the law, must now bring the play to its close among the powers that he has aligned himself with. Perhaps it was with the justification that they might otherwise have simply picked someone else, someone who could have been even worse. In other words, to keep out one villain, just become a villain yourself.

And then, between dances, and with a fanfare from the orchestra, they bring in the prophet's head on a platter.

Herod, are you such a fool, that you can believe that you serve the good powers of life with this evil play? Can you make yourself believe that this will lead to anything but the corruption of the soul, and to damnation in hell for yourself and your misguided people?

And now you, my countrymen, who have been cast into the prisons of the state because you heard the voice of truth, I pray to God that you may be strong and faithful towards the belief that you acted rightly. But if any of you become unsure or doubtful, then I forgive you your sins, on behalf of my Lord Jesus, as He forgave those of John. And you shall know, that He will judge you by your actions, that you stepped bravely forward for the sake of truth, while some lied, and others kept silent. And you shall know that you have helped to bring about that deed from which a healthy future can grow. From the church we can say to you; *The Lord of the truth has let his face shine upon you—He gives you His peace!*

Amen.

The forbidden sermons
#2- May 1943

The Christ Child and Stephen

"Let men stop being animals..."

We have heard so many Christmas sermons that tell us how to share in the joy of Christmas. *Are you alone and sad, my friend, and plagued by doubt and anxiety? Then come, kneel at the manger, and the child will give you peace, and a share of the heavenly joy.* To that there is just one thing to say—We have not been given Jesus to make us happy. We have Ib Schønberg[11] for that. God has not taken on the role of entertainer. It might be true, that to know Jesus is a joy in itself. But if you want to know Jesus so that you can increase your comfort level, then you are guilty of blasphemy. Christ is the object of our faith, and he who will use Him as the means is a blasphemer.

One day the parish pastor went to the doctor's office in town. The doctor's wife opened the door, and her three year old boy, who was tugging at her dress, exclaimed at the sight of the pastor: *Is it Christmas now?* The child believed that the pastor, just like Santa Claus, was an image that only appeared at Christmas. There are many members of the Christian church who think that the pastor and Santa Claus are on the same level, and that the Christmas service is one of the treats that belongs to Christmas Eve. And, together with the many nice and pleasant things that are necessary on that evening of the year, are the oh so sweet stories about the Christ child, and then two spoonful's of the harmless Ingemann[12] melodies, sparkling like pine needles in a Christmas candle.

And if someone is sitting in church, feeling a bit dejected, and can't quite seem to hear the right *Merry Christmas* melody; there is always a pastor who can offer some consolation.

Such a crazy and fateful misunderstanding! The pastor is not there to console us anymore than the gospel is. The pastor and the gospel are there to make us feel the heat of hell. People can console each other, or they can console themselves. Christ was not involved with consolation. The pastor and the gospel are there to show man reality; as I just said, to make us feel the heat of hell. So long as that has not happened, we have no use for heaven.

When so many today feel that the church is completely irrelevant, it is, to a large degree, because its pastors serve up things that people do not know they need. And then they feel as if we are foisting something upon them. They feel as if they live inland, and here we come in a big hurry with cement for building bridges across the water.

Glory be to God in the highest, peace on earth, and good will toward men, sang the heavenly choir. Now what does that mean? Did the angels come down with these gifts that night? Yes and no. They didn't bring them in the sense that they were magically made real: The earth was not suddenly filled with piety, peace, and love of neighbour. No, they brought these gifts, but it was as if they had been dropped like weapons by parachute. Piety, peace, and love of neighbour are what Christ brought to His disciples, so that they could conquer the world with them, and teach the nations how to use them.

The little Christ Child is the world's saviour and the Prince of Peace, because He is the world's greatest warlord. It looks like there is a glaring contrast between the gospel of Christmas Day and the gospel of Saint Stephen's Day: The Christ Child and the first Christian martyr—Stephen. In reality there is a close connection.

The pagan Christmas, with eating and drinking, and family festivities, can easily go together with the Christian, but it can never take its place. Jesus too was a family man. He liked people and parties, and yet walked ever toward the cross. Let us just sing some Ingemann hymns, eat goose, and gather with our children by the glittering toy tree. But let us Christians never forget, that the coming of Christ to earth mandates relentless struggle against evil. And if we kneel at the manger in more than just a sentimental and innocent mood, we will see that one of the Child's hands is open and friendly, and the other is clenched in blood.

The Christian's true Christmas joy has nothing to do with some pleasant and soothing internal voices telling us that we can be so faithful that neither sin nor sorrow nor death can touch us. It's possible that some people have such an unusual personality that they can make themselves believe that, and thank God for it. But that's not Christianity, but hypnosis and make-believe. No, the true Joy of Christmas is the joy of being there where it counts, the pride of being sent to the front lines. Jesus came as a gift to man, that God's front might be established here on earth. He is the Saviour of the world to the same extent that He has conquered it. Christianity is full of unbelievable things: The Trinity, the virgin birth, baptism and the Eucharist are a few of them. But the most unbelievable of them all is, that God needs *me*. It is so unbelievable that it would be blasphemy if God Himself had not told me. Yes, how it pleases me, that such nonsense is life's profoundest wisdom, and that something so incredible can be the basis of my faith.

The church has failed Christianity so often, even betrayed it, by turning it into a redemption club: *What's important for you is to get into heaven, and you can do that by believing this and that, and doing such and such.*

To be a Christian is to feel a bond with Christ—even if you can't explain how or why. Not out of fear of hell, nor to insure your place in heaven. As parents feel a bond with their children, as man feels drawn toward woman, and as the central element in a friendship always has some mystery about it, it is in that way that the Christian feels a bond with his Saviour and Lord. The Christmas gospel tells us about the birth of a man, who, with his mysterious radiance, gathered a congregation of friends about Himself, who persevered through all the challenges, and grew over the centuries, and whose great goal was to conquer the earth, driven by His love, and guided by His strength. The gospel of Saint Stephen's Day tells about one of His first friends, and about how the friends of Jesus were when at their best.

Merry Christmas we wish each other. Which means: I hope you like the roast goose (or meatballs, if you can't afford goose), and hopefully you will have fuel for the stove, and your friends and loved ones will be with you, so that the tree sparkles, and the hymns ring out with their usual power. And may these words, despite all, live in your heart: *I will be there, O Jesus, where Thee wilt have me. But I am full of doubts and questions, and these spoil my Christmas joy.* Well, who said you should have any Christmas joy? Maybe it would be good for you to have a really bad Christmas. Don't think for a minute, you spoiled child, that God is a Christmas elf who has an electromagnet in his sack that He can use to shock your brain cells so that you can understand it all, and have a good time, and be in harmony and in good spirit. My dear friend, you can ask the doctor about that, and he might give you a caffeine prescription; that usually sends blood to your brain, and clears things up so that you feel good again. But that has nothing to do with the true joy of Christmas. The true joy of Christmas—that is when you, no matter how much you understand or not, possess Christ, and will go where He will have you. True Christianity is not just the belief in the virgin birth, or the resurrection; true Christianity means that you are good to your servants. And that doesn't mean that you simply allow them to do anything they want, but that you demand their obedience, yet keep them in your heart.

You have many servants who can help you to live a worthy life. You have, for example, the truth. Be good to it. It is in your daily bread, so that you will use it often. Do not let God see that you hold its service in disdain. The truth may require a sacrifice. It cost Stephen his life. There was another one of our Lord's friends who paid with his life. But that was because he did not serve the truth. His name was Judas Iscariot. Which of those two disciples would you rather be, if it came to that?

Poor Christendom, how often it has failed to grasp Christianity! It sulks if it isn't full of Christmas joy. Without ever having done God's will, it demands God's kindness. One cannot be a murderer, and at the same time have a clean conscience. How can you demand that God should make you happy, O man, you who have never made your neighbour happy? Go first and reconcile with your brother, and then come to the house of God.

I wish you a joyous Christmas, my listener, that Christ may live in your heart, that you may partake of the heavenly host here on earth, whose song is glory to God, peace on earth, and good will toward men. To sing is to strive—for the goal is the spirit in faith to all that is sacred.

Give God honour! Death and corruption over those who wage war upon the world! Let freedom march! Let men stop being animals, and walk forward on the path to become men in the image of God.

Amen

The forbidden sermons
#3- May 1943

Christ and Denmark

Jesus ... who compels me

It is New Year's Day. Not for the church, but for the world. The church has its own New Year on the first Sunday in Advent. Then we sing: *Welcome, to the New Year of Grace, welcome here today.*

The first of January is not a holiday for the church. You can call it a secular holiday. Our thoughts go out from the church to the world, and to our native land. A new year dawns on Denmark today. How has the old year gone? How will the New Year go? What do we have to thank Christ for in the old year, we ask, and what will He demand of us in the New Year?

Many Christians will say: *We thank God that we have been kept out of the war this past year.* I too love my home, my house, my health, my wife, and my children. Nor would I want to see my home in ruins, or my children with limbs ripped off lying in the dust and rubble. And yet there are two things that I would far less want to see, and with God's help will never see. And they are the truth betrayed, and my country's honor sacrificed.

I cannot be among those who are thanking God for having kept us out of the war. First of all, we have not been kept out of it. Our country is occupied. Nobody knows what this blood, fire, and invasion will mean for us. And second, no one can thank God for helping somebody to cheat in a horse trade. God demanded that we fight. We betrayed His command, and we betrayed our own vows and resolutions. One shall not make a fool of God by thanking Him that the devil takes care of his own.

Are these words too strong? No! Those who betray God put themselves under the devil's protection. We have failed our calling and our destiny. Denmark has felt the wrath of God. And that is why we are so well off.

We have shirked our duty. We let others bleed for our sake and our cause. We have sold our soul to the evil spirit of compromise, and signed a contract with the blood of others. That is why everything goes so well for us.

The pen burns in my hand like a red-hot iron as I write these words. But I will endure this ordeal by fire. Why? Because I am a Christian, because I stand at the pulpit, and because today the gospel speaks the name of Jesus. He is the One who drives me forth.

Where is our people's struggle for the faith they until now have invoked? Where is their sacrifice for the ideals that they would want to be victorious?

Don't believe what the politicians say when they praise us. There are many good and honorable men among them. The Danish members of parliament are among the best in the world, as far as clean hands go. They are without lust for power, and even more free of corruption. But they see their duty not in leading, but in being led. Their existence as politicians, according to the rules of the game, depends on them praising the people, the voters. Do not trust them! They are feathering their own nests.

And don't trust those in the folk high schools. Alas, where is the red faith, and the white rage of the high schools in this black night? One would think they were the old age children of Grundtvig, sired when he was more senile then he ever did become. It was Pastor Bartholdy of the Inner Mission who said the words that the folk high schools should have said, and that Grundtvig would have said, if he had been alive among us. There are high schools where one can hear the sharp clang of the sword, and thank God for them! Yet they are the schools that have trouble making a go of it.

And don't put too much faith in the pastors. They are too poorly paid, and they have been educated in the humanities. They have forgotten, or never learned, what Christianity is. They have been bottle-fed love, and in a world of men they speak too often of the effeminate. They say *stay out of politics*. They preach peace at any price, in support of the devil, who would like to see that evil is allowed to spread. Scripture does not say: If your neighbour is struck upon one cheek, then it is your duty to hold him so that he can be struck upon the other as well. Do not trust the preachers until they wake up and remember that they are servants for the entire gospel, for the Prince of Peace who came not to bring peace, but the sword, for Him who forgave Peter and let Judas hang himself, for Him who was meek and humble of heart, and yet drove the blasphemers from the temple.

And do not trust the *majority*, for they have a herd mentality, and are easy to fool. The masses regale themselves with the praises they hear about their self-discipline, exceptional solidarity, and high culture. How much of their self-discipline is cowardice? And is their solidarity more that just playing dead, and their high culture more than just bowing for those who kick down the door? Do not trust the neglected masses! I think they are good enough at their core, but that core lies deep, deep down. They are pampered and spoiled. When have we seen within us the will and courage to *demand* something of our people? The prime minister, who was buried at public expense, never tired of emphasizing, that when it came to *our* life and *our* honor, although others fought and suffered for theirs, we made sure to keep our buildings undamaged, and our skin without a scratch. What fools (we would have to conclude), in those other countries that fought! Our greatest poet of today, whose books are in such high demand, regales the populace with sunshine stories about how things always end so well in this wonderful world of ours. And one of our most popular lyricists, a truly great poet, has been breast-feeding our people with his ditty:

> *Dinge-a-ling a-ling*
> *We'll play a game today*
> *Dinge-a-ling a-lay*
> *A game for us today*

Well, that game became an expensive one for us!

Haven't we done anything at all so that we can meet our fate with our heads held high? Sure, we have arranged meetings for our youth where some older people came and sang patriotic songs. They could then go home, having done their patriotic duty.

Otherwise our people have allowed themselves to be stripped of power, seeing those men removed from parliament who they would have kept, and those who they least wanted, retained, while others who nobody wanted or had trust in, were put in office.

And meanwhile our police force has grown out of proportion, and our courts seem to have forgotten the constitution.

Alas, how dutifully they have been squirming in the dust—the editors and directors. There are many who care, but few who dare. The free Danish people has, without lifting a finger, allowed itself to be enslaved, while those who fight can mock them—*Better a slave in the ashes, than a hero in the cemetery.*

Every large party or event begins with a speech bemoaning the present difficult conditions, and expressing the meekest wish that we might soon get our freedom and independence back, *like they had promised.* Then the party begins with plenty of eating and drinking, and a band playing. The youth of other countries, their bodies, lie rotting on the field of battle, while the souls of our youth lie rotting in the dance halls.

We don't dare demand anything from them, because we don't dare demand anything from ourselves. We are up to our necks in materialism, we don't believe a word of the gospel, or that the soul is more than the body. And it is so easy to close a meeting with the short verse:

> *Fight for all that you hold dear,*
> *Die, if that's what's needed!*

We like to sing that verse, but to mean it, to live by it? God forbid! —And once again: God forbid!

And there are those who protest, those who really want to do something, those who know that youth is corrupted if it is forced into passiveness, and that the country will be cheated out of its future if one only thinks about the present. And there are those who stand up against obedience and double play—what happens to them? Against the constitution, against the people's sense of justice, and against justice itself, but in obedience to foreign demands, their own countrymen throw them in prison. So many of Denmark's best men and women have now been attacked, deported, and driven into exile, that we can just as well say that there is now a civil war being waged.

Henrik Ibsen[13] wanted to teach the Norwegian people to think large. Our poets, our leaders, have taught us nonsense and supplication. *It's too bad for the young with that compulsory military service, and it's too bad for the young that they have to abstain until marriage.* We were that people in Europe who were best off, and still we thought that it was too bad for us that we even existed.

Think large? Did Ibsen succeed in teaching his people that? Yes, look at the Norwegian people today! Their courage and strength shine out across the world. And how the Danish church has admired its brother church in Norway for its strength and vision! The Finnish people, the Norwegian people, neither of them greater than us—and yet how very much greater!

What do we Danes have to cling to? Our past? That is worth nothing if it is not alive in us today.

Our constitution? That is only good for a people who are determined to respect it, and who demand that it be respected.

Our king? He is no longer young, and illness and bad luck have been hard on him. And yet he is our symbol of unity, and he has our full devotion. But he is only one. And what of the men who surround him?

There is a story about a woman from the island of Funen. She was a member of a church council, who in bewilderment blurted out: *Well, that's terrible; it looks like we only have our Lord to rely on.*

That's how *terrible* our situation is today. We only have our Lord to rely on. Thank God for Him! Praise God that we have God, whose wrath is also His grace, who forgives the sins of a nation, and gives strength so that we again can be as young as an eagle.

That is what our ancient nation needs: the power of rejuvenation, God's rejuvenating power, so a new nation can appear, though it be the old one: the worthy sons of the father. The gospel will teach the Danish people to think as a great people. To choose honor before profit, freedom before well-paid bondage, to believe that victory comes out of sacrifice, that life comes out of death, and the future from devotion—in short, to believe in Christ: what does it benefit a people, if it gains the world, but loses its soul?

The cross in our flag—it's been a long time since we've realized that it means something. And yet it is the cross that characterizes the Scandinavian flags. We have crept into the church, the few of us who go there, and heard about the cross, about Christ's suffering, and Christ's demand for self-sacrifice and struggle. And we thought that we should understand that in a spiritual sense, but not that it applied to us today. We were Christians when we sat in the church and sang Amen—but no, no, we are first Christians when we go out into the world and say no to the devil and all his doing, and say yes to the Holy Spirit.

And this is what the church demands of you this New Year's Day. You men in the Danish government, if you will be the government of a Christian nation, that in the year to come you will act with Christ's spirit of strength and love. We know that your task is gigantically difficult. But if you act in God's spirit, He, who is superior to the giants, will give you steadfastness, wisdom, and strength.

Our people are being divided more and more into rich and poor. You must pursue the ill gained riches of war with Christian ruthlessness, so that those who earn blood money are hit with taxes so that they themselves bleed, and their money is distributed to the thousands who cringe under inflation and the swindle of substitute commodities. You must watch over our youth who are daily brutalized and trivialized. Hold accountable those parents who do not keep their children safe from vermin and sexual diseases, or allow them to run all hours of the night to their life-long detriment. You must remain true to the divine ideals of democracy. Do not make victims of conscience, do not persecute other faiths, grant all people access to justice, and avoid at all costs persecution of the weak. And never forget that you are the guardians of the crown jewels of a millennial kingdom, not just for today, but for a millennial future, and that the three greatest of those jewels are: Honor, honor, and honor. These are the first and the last, and if you cannot watch over them, then it would be better that you didn't even exist.

The snow is melting, the fog is lifting, and before us there lies a land that will again grow green. We love it beyond words. We love it because it is Denmark. We love it for Rolf's bravery, for Thyra's foresight, for Absalon's Viking Christianity, for Margrethe's vision and noble soul, for Christian 4th's faithful work, for the south Jutlandic farmer's endurance and unshakeable faith, for our mother's worn working hands, and for our loved one's midsummer night's kiss. We love it for the sake of its fresh capital city, for Funen's unique beauty, and for Jutland, so much like England. And for all of the small islands and for the sea, which is our kingdom, from our rivers to the end of the world.

We love this land for her poets and thinkers, for the Dalgas's, for the dairies, for the Danish worker, who without complaint carries the day's burdens on his broad back, and for the foot soldier, who from the day of Sweyn Forkbeard[14] up to Christian 10th, tells his jokes even in death. We love this land because her children's cheeks are red and round, because she has taught us to be good to animals, and to treat each other like human beings, because we have all been brought up with a Nordic sense of chivalry, and contempt for tormentors.

We love this land when she prospers and laughs, and tells the world adventures that are true, but most of all we love this land when she has fallen and lies immobilized in shame, because...we failed. Oh, Mother, forgive us!

Millennia lie before us. Should our children, and their children in turn, think back on this time, and think about us, in such a way that we must blush in our graves.

No! And so we pray: Give us Christianity, give us courage, and give us the faith to lift ourselves up from despondency and fickleness, to do the right thing, regardless of the price. Because betrayal of our ideals can have the most dangerous consequences for our land and people. May we have the courage to regain faith in that which we believed in, even if the prisons fill to overflowing? Those who have willingly shaven their necks to honor the philistines must be able to turn the mills in Gaza long enough that their hair will again grow out.

May the cross in our flag lead us to fight with the imprisoned Norway and the bleeding Finland in the struggle of the North against the idea that is against all of ours, and lead ancient Denmark forth to its new spirit. Not by the grace or promises of others shall our flag again be free, as only God can grant freedom, and He gives it only to those who know that it is a gift that carries an obligation. May the cross in our flag lead us forward to join the other flags of the North! With renewed honor, and restored freedom, the ancient Denmark in the young North—that vision shall shine for us on this New Year's day. We, who see it, will dedicate ourselves to it. We promise that we will. God hear our prayer, and say your own Amen.

29 August 1943
Denmark revolts
Acts 27:7—28,1

Today is a proud day for Denmark

That which we have suffered under so terribly during the last three or four years—our vacillation and our lip service to injustice—now seems to be coming to an end. Again and again, serious Christians have had to ask themselves: Have we been left completely outside of God's plan these years? And we knew that to be a danger far greater than just our hostility toward Germany. Surely we will get over the second one, but never over the first.

Now we can breathe a sigh of relief, and greet each other with a *congratulations countryman*. Now our position is clear. If we have the will, then the best thing has happened to us: now we are in God's hands. We will no longer try to get by with tricks, excuses, and duplicity. Now, with the grace of God, we throw ourselves into His living hands. There will be suffering, and blood will flow —that has always been a part of being a child of God. Finally we Danes can begin to sing, *A Mighty Fortress is our God, Our strong and sure protection*. Though God is all-powerful, He can only save those people for whom He is a fortress.

Before coming to church today, I did something that I normally never do. I opened the Bible to a random page, and now I'll read to you what I found there—

> *And when we had sailed slowly many days, and scarce were come over against Cnidus, the wind not suffering us, we sailed under Crete, over against Salmone; And, hardly passing it, came unto a place which is called The fair havens; nigh whereunto was the city of Lasea. Now when much time was spent, and when sailing was now dangerous, because the fast was now already past,*

Paul admonished them, And said unto them, Sirs, I perceive that this voyage will be with hurt and much damage, not only of the lading and ship, but also of our lives. Nevertheless the centurion believed the master and the owner of the ship, more than those things which were spoken by Paul. And because the haven was not commodious to winter in, the more part advised to depart thence also, if by any means they might attain to Phenice, and there to winter; which is an haven of Crete, and lieth toward the south west and north west.

And when the south wind blew softly, supposing that they had obtained their purpose, loosing thence, they sailed close by Crete. But not long after there arose against it a tempestuous wind, called Euroclydon. And when the ship was caught, and could not bear up into the wind, we let her drive. And running under a certain island which is called Clauda, we had much work to come by the boat: Which when they had taken up, they used helps, undergirding the ship; and, fearing lest they should fall into the quicksands, strake sail, and so were driven. And we being exceedingly tossed with a tempest, the next day they lightened the ship; And the third day we cast out with our own hands the tackling of the ship. And when neither sun nor stars in many days appeared, and no small tempest lay on us, all hope that we should be saved was then taken away.

But after long abstinence Paul stood forth in the midst of them, and said, Sirs, ye should have hearkened unto me, and not have loosed from Crete, and to have gained this harm and loss. And now I exhort you to be of good cheer: for there shall be no loss of any man's life among you, but of the ship. For there stood by me this night the angel of God, whose I am, and whom I serve, Saying, Fear not, Paul; thou must be brought before Caesar: and, lo, God hath given thee all them that sail with thee. Wherefore, sirs, be of good cheer: for I believe God, that it shall be even as it was told me. Howbeit we must be cast upon a certain island.

But when the fourteenth night was come, as we were driven up and down in Adria, about midnight the shipmen deemed that they drew near to some country; And sounded, and found it twenty fathoms: and when they had gone a little further, they sounded again, and found it fifteen fathoms. Then fearing lest we should have fallen upon rocks, they cast four anchors out of the stern, and wished for the day.

And as the shipmen were about to flee out of the ship, when they had let down the boat into the sea, under colour as though they would have cast anchors out of the foreship, Paul said to the centurion and to the soldiers, Except these abide in the ship, ye cannot be saved.

Then the soldiers cut off the ropes of the boat, and let her fall off. And while the day was coming on, Paul besought them all to take meat, saying, This day is the fourteenth day that ye have tarried and continued fasting, having taken nothing. Wherefore I pray you to take some meat: for this is for your health: for there shall not an hair fall from the head of any of you. And when he had thus spoken, he took bread, and gave thanks to God in presence of them all: and when he had broken it, he began to eat. Then were they all of good cheer, and they also took some meat. And we were in all in the ship two hundred threescore and sixteen souls.

And when they had eaten enough, they lightened the ship, and cast out the wheat into the sea. And when it was day, they knew not the land: but they discovered a certain creek with a shore, into the which they were minded, if it were possible, to thrust in the ship. And when they had taken up the anchors, they committed themselves unto the sea, and loosed the rudder bands, and hoisted up the mainsail to the wind, and made *toward shore And falling into a place where two seas met, they ran the ship aground; and the forepart stuck fast, and remained immoveable, but the hinder part was broken with the violence of the waves. And the soldiers' counsel was to kill the prisoners, lest any of them should swim out, and escape. But the centurion, willing to save Paul, kept them from their purpose; and commanded that they which could swim should cast themselves first into the sea, and get to land: And the rest, some on boards, and some on broken pieces of the ship. And so it came to pass, that they escaped all safe to land. And when they were escaped, then they knew that the island was called Melita.*

(While reading I emphasized the great difficulty of the passage, and that the worldly captain of the ship would not believe the words of the apostle. And how Paul's conviction grew, even while the situation worsened. The words: "We shall be cast upon a certain island," I understood to mean—an island shall save us.

And the Island was called Malta, and they were good and helpful people who took care of those who had so bravely survived the many dangers.)

The sermon ended with a prayer, that God would send an angel to King Christian, preferably one of the great angels, an archangel, most preferably Uriah—he who brings light.

December 5, 1943
2nd Sunday in Advent
Matthew 25: 1-13

Sermon in Copenhagen Cathedral

Then shall the kingdom of heaven be likened unto ten virgins, who took their lamps, and went forth to meet the bridegroom. And five of them were wise, and five were foolish. Those who were foolish took their lamps, and took no oil with them: But the wise took oil in their vessels with their lamps. While the bridegroom tarried, they all slumbered and slept. And at midnight there was a cry made, Behold, the bridegroom cometh; go ye out to meet him. Then all those virgins arose, and trimmed their lamps. And the foolish said unto the wise, Give us of your oil; for our lamps are gone out.

But the wise answered, saying, Not so; lest there be not enough for us and you: but go ye rather to them that sell, and buy for yourselves. And while they went to buy, the bridegroom came; and they that were ready went in with him to the marriage: and the door was shut. Afterward came also the other virgins, saying, Lord, Lord, open to us. But he answered and said, Verily I say unto you, I know you not. Watch therefore, for ye know neither the day nor the hour wherein the Son of man cometh.

The great powers are engaged in a struggle for life or death. And so too is that great power we call the church. For the church is a great power, greater than the others. The others fight for themselves, for their own existence. The church is a great power, and its goals are much greater. It is fighting for the soul of mankind. If it only fights for itself it is doomed. You are not here for your own sake—and the church is not here for its own sake either. If it were to only think of itself, instead of its mission, then we could just as well let the Russians come and take it.

When I was a child I understood that the story of the ten virgins was a simple warning, that if we did not give ourselves to the Lord, then we were doomed. And it is probably true that that was a part of the story. There are many directions in the church other than the evangelical, and they are fully justified. But there must always be evangelism within the church. There is something seriously wrong with a church that does not bear this witness:

You must profess your Christianity; you must give yourself to God with all that your are and all that you possess; God calls upon you to give yourself to Him, to take leave of yourself in an act of willful mysticism—if you do not give yourself to God, then you cannot enter the Kingdom of heaven.

Have you in earnest heard the cry: *The bridegroom is coming?* And if you do not go forth to meet him, then you will learn, you pitiful soul, that on the morning of the resurrection you will be standing before a closed door. And although it's true that God's mercy is boundless, it is for just that reason it is so serious. If you push Him away from you, then you will experience that the God of mercy is merciless through His mercy—for the drama of Golgotha was bloody reality, and not just a theatrical play that one can attend, or not, as one pleases.

And I repeat: this message must always be heard in the church that carries the name of Jesus.

But quite often we make ourselves believe that *Christianity is a matter between God and me.* If I have given my heart to God, then I know that I am a faithful Christian, and that I have received forgiveness for my sins through the blood that was sacrificed for me. And then I can revel in uplifting thoughts that now, thank

God, I am safe, and others can figure out how to manage this on their own.

That which has shaken me the most in the story that our Lord is telling us today is that they have all fallen asleep. The foolish virgins—they might just sleep in, going with the flow, thinking: It will all work out in the end. But the wise virgins—they too have allowed themselves to be caught off guard by their belief that they had their affairs in order. Well, they did get through the door, but they had to leave their friends behind. The bridegroom got a sleepy reception. And the story ends with the muffled sound of small, sweaty, panic stricken hands of girls scratching at the closed door—and the stern voice within—and it is the merciful God's stern voice: *Verily I say unto you, I know you not.*

That is a very blunt story that describes our situation, as are many of those by the gentle Saviour. The only thing enlightening about it is—that it is not enlightening!

Because it is in fact the story about our situation today. Can't you hear it? It calls down to us from heaven: What did I say? It was bitter and heavy, and it was eternally serious: What did I say? There were ten virgins, and they all fell asleep. Just because My arrival was delayed, My entire church fell asleep.

For that is the truth about us. And that applies from the pope in Rome to the parish pastor here in Vedersø: we have fallen asleep, because the second coming of Christ is dragging out. In plain Danish, Christ is not alive enough for us, and that which we preach is the message, instead of the reality. There was a doctor in central Jutland who was at a meeting of believers. He stood up and proposed a toast: Shall we toast Hitler? Now, that was long before 9th April [15]. Some at the meeting protested, and the doctor shouted back: *There are hundreds of thousands who are ready to give their lives for Hitler, how many of you Christians will do that for Christ?*

That story really hit me hard. That the church has stood relatively weak in the onslaught of new religions is not the fault of the church's Master—He is the same as always—it is our fault, the church's fault, which has lost its second most precious treasure. The most precious is Christ Himself, but the second most precious is martyrdom—Christian martyrdom. Not that they were heroes, or were possessed by ambition, and not that they were sick at heart and enjoyed torturing themselves—but that they loved Christ so much that no sacrifice for Him was too great. With this martyrdom we once won over the world, and without it the world will win over us. The Romans thought that if only they killed the Christians, then they would be dead. But the blood of the Christians was like seed.

We talk about freethinkers, about the new sexual morals, the curse of technology, and the materialism of youth. But all of that is meaningless. We must turn the spotlight upon ourselves. The first Christians were backward in comparison to us; they were poor, superstitious, had little knowledge of medicine, and were poor preachers. Paul, for example, suffered from that terrible habit of never being able to finish talking, or as they say in Jutland, he couldn't find *Amen*, and people would fall asleep. But Christ was the living reality for them. He had called down a storm of misfortunes over them; even that much courage He had. One sometimes hears nice young people today say: yes, we would dare to risk something ourselves, but it will just hurt others. And so they do nothing for the sake of those others. Christ was a warrior; he stood in the forward ranks, and did not shy away from leading His men forward to where death and mutilation would be the wages of heroism. And they went, without hesitation, proudly. *So happy to be disgraced for His sake.* Oh, my Christian friends, that is where we must go. Not for our own sake, not to secure a ticket to a seat in heaven. But because we are Christians, no matter how lukewarm or sleepy we are, we are Christians—which means we have been entrusted with the kingdom.

That was the message that Christ brought to mankind, and that was the sacrifice he gave for it. The intention was, after all, not just to get a few rapacious souls to take out an insurance policy for salvation. Paul was not right—as far as I can see—that we Christians are the unhappiest of all people, if there is not more than just this life on earth. Jesus too was very much on this side of life. His declaration was: *Thy kingdom come, Thy will be done, on earth as it in heaven*. Those brides, who had taken their lamps, and then gone forth to meet the bridegroom, they really were His congregation here on earth, and "to go forth to meet Him" is a parable for joining the struggle to establish His kingdom here on earth. And therefore Drachmann[16] has a reason to be angry: If we pastors just issue promissory notes on eternity, then we are not His pastors, He who never issued promissory notes, but created eternity wherever He went. Christianity was in reality always a rather unspiritual religion. The carpenter's son from Nazareth, being the good Jew that he was, never betrayed the earth. The earth, created by God the Father, corrupted by evil, and yet created by God the Father with Himself as its goal. This goal would be the work of the Son to fulfill. And so it must be said as clearly as possible, that when the pious Christians complain over the preaching of politics in church, then they are engaging in unchristian speech.

Well— *Let's keep politics out of the church,* some say, *we hear enough of politics on the radio, and we read about it in the newspapers. Let's be free of that in the house of God.* But how is it that we hear about it on the radio, and read about in the papers? Perhaps we should hear about it in God's house, but in a different way than we are used to. In God's house we should hear about politics judged in relation to the word of God. It is well enough to have your salvation taken care of, and to be sure in your faith, and all of that which belongs to the imagination and spirit. But I will never forget what the dear teacher from my youth, Professor Geismar[17], once told me: he had participated in a large open air gathering of Christians in Germany, and after they had talked each other into a frenzy, to the point where the entire crowd believed that they had only to get down on their knees and pray, and that a miracle would take place, with voices in tongues, and the outpouring of the holy spirit, and Christ in the cloud, then an Englishman shouted out over their heads, in poor German: *Wir mussen Gottes Wille tun (We need to do God's will.)*

The world powers agree with the pious Christians, that politics should not be discussed in Church. And the church would gladly serve them in that way, if only they would practice politics in a manner that is not against the teachings of Christ. But if they follow a path in politics that Christ has shown to be against the will of God, and therefore leads the people into an abyss, then the church is not the Church of Christ if it remains silent. To be silent about sin is to speak the language of the devil. When Christ railed against the rich, when He excoriated the Pharisees, He was dealing with financial and legal matters. When the Christians refused to make a sacrifice to the image of Caesar, they were in open revolt. God forgive us, if we don't understand, that that is what the church is for: at any given moment to make eternity relevant. It would be going too far in this sermon to get into details. But I will name one. When here at home a certain group of our countrymen is persecuted just because of their heritage, then it is the Christian's duty to speak up: *this is against the constitution of God's kingdom, the rule of compassion, and it is repulsive to the free Nordic mind.* And the church must go even further, and never grow weary. If it happens once more, then with God's help we will lead our people to revolt. For a Christian people, who sit idly by while its ideals are trampled under foot, is allowing a cancerous decay to grow in its mind, and the wrath of God will be upon it.

Our people! Our people! We are a Christian Danish congregation, and as Christians the fate of our people cannot be irrelevant to us. There is something in the parable today that strikes hard at us, not just as Christians, but also as a people. We are an enterprising and vigilant people in many ways, but concerning the very question of existence, we are a strangely complacent people.

There was a cry at midnight. It was not: the bridegroom is coming; it was: The wolf is coming. The war broke out upon us. And we did not have oil for our lamps, and those who we could have borrowed from stayed away, as they always do, from those who could have made preparations, but did not. We can feel chilled through to the bone out of fear that the Danish people, in reward for its complacency, will be left standing outside the gates of life, and life's stern Lord, who demands struggle and sacrifice from his people, shall answer our cry: *Verily I say unto you, I know you not.* But we pray that some changes can be made to this parable—and that we may be granted a moment of mercy in which to obtain oil for our lamp.

And let us not believe those who preach only despair and condemnation over us. There are many clear signs that the Danish people are starting to awake from their spiritual sleep. And even if people with warped concepts of honor give lectures, and distribute brochures, the Danish people have at least kept a clear head. And when the audience at the Royal Theater praises Ewald's[18] tale of the fisherman, it's not just praise for the refreshing way the young actor sings, it's not just a salute to the dead poet and his great gift to the people, and it's not just in gratitude and honor to King Christian, who is our King Christian—it is all of that, but it is also more. It is in gratitude to the Danish navy, which has always been worthy of the words of our national anthem. And it is a prayer that we all may regain the spirit that filled the arthritic poet in his life's two high points; when he, with the song *King Christian stood by the lofty mast,* strode toward an honorable grave, and when he, with the help of the Saviour, crossed over that final bridge: *Take up arms, hero of Golgotha.*

We hear many harsh words about the youth of our time, and some of them are justified. But with that said, we must also remember that there are many young people who are fresh, healthy, and active, and in their own way hold the highest ideals—a youth we admire, not because it's young, but because it's young in the right way, it's true to its family, it is at home in its work, and over and over again has shown undaunted courage and bravery—ready to risk life, limb, and honor for its country.

The church will awaken Denmark, as a nation, but it will not at any price get by with that awakening alone. Nationalism without Christianity we condemn as an evil. Hatred spreads across the world, with a savage and corrosive evil. Christ has taught us something larger: with all our abilities and strength to stand up against evil without hatred, not to be weakened by hatred. Christ has taught us the deep difference between just punishment and revenge. When this war has reached its bloody end, the Prince of darkness will cry out for revenge from the grave. And we too know people who must be dealt with. But it shall be done in the spirit of God, and not in the spirit of the devil. May we each be ready, in that station in which we each stand, and with the ability we each have—and without a thought to what it will cost us—to take our turn to help the world move forward, toward the coming of His kingdom, and the victory of His will here on earth, as it is in His eternal heaven.

New Year's Day
Saturday, 1944

Kaj Munk's Last Sermon

Dear Lord and Father in heaven, we thank You for having built Your house here on earth, so that the truth could have such a mighty fortress here among us. And we thank You because You have called us here on this New Year's Day of 1944. There are so many who lie in this world. But here Your word is heard, and it does not ask for applause, nor speak with anger, but is just as sure to comfort as to chastise. If only we would live by it.

Amen

Dear parishioners here in Vedersø! First I want to say thank you for the good Christmas offering of 260 kroner. It will be distributed with one-third to the Bible Society, and two-thirds to the nursing homes of Ringkøbing County.

You are probably wondering why I am standing here below the pulpit, next to the Christmas tree, in my overcoat, and with my bright red scarf around my neck. Yesterday, while I was preparing myself to see the face of God at this service, I realized that I could not ascend to the pulpit, or stand before the altar today. A deep sorrow and pain has filled my heart. In recent times there has been a breach in the good national solidarity in our parish. There are those who, without needing to, place themselves at the service of the Germans. This must, in the name of truth, be spoken about in this church, which was built to be a fortress for the truth. Some believe that such talk does not belong in the House of God. That is wrong. When people in this parish sin, the parish has its house of God so that that can be denounced. The word of God cannot be confined within certain limits. It applies to all aspects of our entire life.

Denmark is at war with Germany. Until August 29th we could have said that our position was not clear. On that day the German commander in Denmark based his actions on principles that only apply to countries at war. For that reason, when a Dane voluntarily helps a German now, then it is an act of treason.

I do not stand here to preach hatred against anyone. That is quite impossible for me. I don't even hate Adolf Hitler. I know what terror and misery the world has been cast into. I know what degradation my own country has experienced. For months now I have not been able to go to sleep at night without wondering: *Will they come for me tonight?* And that thought is not pleasant for one who loves life, and has enough to do in his calling, and loves his wife and children. And still I cannot hate. Because there are so many different types of men, possessed of so many different spirits, and the Saviour has taught us the prayer: *Forgive them, for they know not what they do.*

But it can never be a Christian act to help the Germans build fortifications against the English so that our own country can be kept in bondage and subjugation as long as possible. And it will never be a Christian act to sell at high prices to the Germans the eggs and meat that our own poor working people in the cities so badly need. And it will never be a Christian act to be at the service of injustice, whether it is out of cowardice, greed, or just convenient compliance.

We know how things have been between these Germans and us. They signed a non-aggression treaty with us. And then they invaded us with their canon, tanks, and airplanes, and made us homeless in our own country, and without justice under our own government. Twice they have shed the blood of our youth, they have stripped our old king of his power, and placed him under surveillance. They have run amok with cruelty and incarceration, and have let loose the plague of Jewish persecution, even in our Nordic land. They have carried off hundred-year-old women, and dragged people by their feet down from second floors with their heads bumping on the steps.

There are many, many good Germans, thank God for that, for otherwise the world would be without hope. Many decent boys have put on the uniform, as decent as our own boys. But as long as they accept that this regime, that they have pledged themselves to, retains power over them, then they must stand shoulder to shoulder with it. If the man in a family drinks, then it affects the whole family. And that is just the way it is. One cannot be complicit in acting like a wolf towards others, and then expect to be treated like an innocent lamb. It is the brutal truth of war, that as long as it continues then it is not people we are dealing with, but uniforms. When we see a German soldier in Denmark, then we must say: that is a uniform—and we must remember what that uniform stands for.

I must tell you that an unspeakable anguish has filled my heart, because among my parishioners are some who have forgotten their Danish Christian duty.

In the old days we used to say that when a sharecropper plowed on Sunday with horses he had borrowed from the farm, then God turned a blind eye. Well, there might be a poor soul, with a wife and children, and nowhere in these hard times to get a piece of bread. Then perhaps God is merciful, and turns a blind eye. And perhaps it happens, that they turn up and put a gun to our temple, or chest, or stomach. We know that such things did not frighten Jesus and his brave disciples. They would have preferred to die rather than being frightened into doing that which was against their conscience. But we are simple people. And maybe we can hope that here too God will turn a blind eye. But when Danish men, without urgent need, and of their own free will, betray their fatherland and Christianity out of simple greed, then the church must tell them that the wealth that they accumulate in that way is blood money, and it will be their damnation.

During recent days 1500 students from our brother land Norway have been sent to abuse and death in German concentration camps. And here in Denmark we risk nothing for our country, our faith, or our ideals. We hear it said so often that freedom fighters are criminals, and that their actions will just end up hurting all of us. We call them communists. They are not communists. Some of them might be. But they are all kinds of people. And they are Danish. There is the son of a bishop, the son of a professor, of a good sharecropper, of a tradesman. It is the youth of the country who we cheated out of fighting. We gave them an education, and then deserted them, though they were ready for any challenge. We left them standing to be made fun of. Yet they are the ones who are showing Denmark's face. With exceptional skill, and thoughtfulness that reaches heaven. Almost no Danish lives have been lost, while they continue to risk life and limb—to risk even more than just their lives. In the question of right or wrong, one should never ask if it's worth it, for that is the devil's doing. But it is worth it! *It will just end up hurting us.* No—and again no! Doing nothing has already hurt us. If we had not ourselves gotten rid of the worst of the factories then we would have been carpet bombed a long time ago. And if we had continued the comedy, smiling at the enemy's evil play, then we would have simply been hitching our little wagon to Germany's great machine on its calamitous fall down the mountainside.

We are not, as they believe, an ageing population that must take what is offered, and do as it is told. Today it is the twentieth anniversary of my first having ascended the pulpit here; and I now stand here below it. I had not thought that this jubilee would be celebrated in this way.

Twenty years—and many memories stand out, and I owe you many thanks for your loyalty, and for your tolerance of me, who has had his own ways, and has been so different from all of you here. So it is that much more painful for me, that which has occurred during this time. I don't know names, and don't want to know them. I can only pray to God that these parishioners will wake up to the truth, look into their own hearts, and find their place as good Christian men among us once again.

Amen

* * *

(Three days later— 4th January 1944, they came after him, and murdered him at Hørbylunde Hills west of Silkeborg. A granite cross now marks the spot where Kaj Munk's body was found. There is no inscription on it. Everyone knows the name.)

The granite cross at Hørbylunde

Works in English by and about Kaj Munk

Five Plays by Kaj Munk
Translated from the Danish by R.P. Keigwin
Nyt Nordisk Forlag Arnold Busck 1964, The American Scandinavian Foundation
Contents: Herod the King; The Word; Cant; He Sits at the Melting Pot; Before Cannae.

Niels Ebbesen by Kaj Munk
Translated into English by Arense Lund with Dave Carley
December 2006 (straight translation and an adaptation)

Niels Ebbesen: Historical Drama in 5 Acts: Translated from Danish by Erna Voight and H. Orlo Miller
The Scandinavian News, Sept. 1942-Feb. 1943

Christianity and Resistance in the 20th Century
From Kaj Munk and Dietrich Bonhoeffer to Desmond Tutu, Brill 2006

Kaj Munk: Playwright, Priest and Patriot,
Translated and edited by R.P. Keigwin
The Free Danish Publishing Company, 1944

Scandinavian Plays of the Twentieth Century
Princeton University Press, The American Scandinavian Foundation, New York 1944;

The Honourable Justice, translated by R.P. Keigwin, 1952

Egelykke
A drama in five acts, translated by Llewellyn Jones, 1954

Modern Scandinavian Plays
Strindberg, August, New York,
Liveright Pub. Corp. 1954, Including Kaj Munk's play *Egelykke*.

Swans of the North: and short stories by modern Danish authors, by Heepe, Evelyn, G.E.C. Gad, Copenhagen 1953, comprising Kaj Munk's: *But it's not like him!*

By The Rivers of Babylon
Kaj Munk – 15 sermons, Translated by John M. Jensen
Lutheran Publishing House
Blair, Nebraska 1945

Four Sermons
by Kaj Munk, Translated by John M. Jensen
Lutheran Publishing House
Blair, Nebraska 1944

Kaj Munk and Germany
Søren Daugbjerg, Aalborg University Press 2008
Translated by Brian Young, New Nordic Press 2011

Endnotes

1 Steen Steensen Blicher, Danish pastor and author (1782-1848), best known for his descriptions of Jutlandic culture. One of the few English translations of his work is "The Diary of a Parish Clerk," Mermaid Press 1991.

2 N.F.S. Grundtvig, Danish author, theologian, pastor, and poet (1783-1872). He wrote many of the hymns in the Danish hymnal. "Danish Fairy Tales" (in English) by Svend Grundtvig, University of Michigan 1914.

3 The description of the "upside down" beer crate is, in Danish, a play on words. The Danish word for "convert", in the religious sense, is "omvende." The word for "turned upside down" is "Omvendt."

4 Landet is the parish on the island of Lolland where Kaj Munk spent his childhood.

5 Valdemarsdag is the Danish Flag Day. According to myth, the Danish flag fell down from heaven in 1219, when King Valdemar fought against Estonia. It is also celebrated for the reunion of North Slesvig with Denmark in 1920.

6 Worms, a German city on the Rhine River. It was in Worms that Martin Luther published his "Ninety-Five theses" in 1520, in protest against the practice of the Catholic Church of selling indulgences. He also translated the Bible into German.

7 Christian Berg, school superintendent and politician (1829-1891).

8 Nis Petersen, Danish author and poet, Kaj Munk's cousin (1897-1943). There are several English translations of his work, best known being "The Street of the Sandal Makers, a tale of Rome in the Time of Marcus Aurelius."

9 Niels Ebbesen, Danish national hero (1308-1340). He led the attack against the bald count Gerhard, the German nobleman who had laid claim to Jutland and Funen. Gerhard was killed at Randers in an attack at night. Kaj Munk wrote a Play, "Niels Ebbesen," based on his life, but really aimed at the occupiers. It was written in 1942, and dedicated to "Our young troops of April 9th." The Germans banned it, and it was illegal to stage the play during the occupation.

10 The Danish word for a branch or twig is "kvist" (can also mean attic). The word used in the original is "Kvistling," obviously a word play referring to the Norwegian traitor Quisling.

11 Ib Schoenberg, a well-known Danish film actor (1902-1955).

12 B.S. Ingemann, Danish hymnist and author (1789-1862). Especially well known for his hymns for children.

13 Henrik Ibsen, Norwegian playwright and poet (1828-1906). Known worldwide through the many translation of his work into English. "A Dolls House" is one of his best-known plays. He is considered to be one of the founders of Modernism in the theater.

14 Sweyn Forkbeard (Sven Tveskæg) was king of Denmark and England (960-1014). He was one of the great Viking kings. After attacking England in 1003 he demanded the reparations known as the Danegæld. His father was Harold Bluetooth (Blåtand).

15 April 9th, 1940 was the day the German army invaded and occupied Denmark.

16 Holger Drachmann, Danish poet and painter (1846-1908)

17 Professor Oscar Geismar, Danish pastor and author (1877-1950). He was inspired by Grundtvig, and in turn was a key figure in the early life of Kaj Munk. He was the local pastor when Kaj Munk was growing up in the village of Opager west of Maribo.

18 Johannes Ewald, Danish dramatist and poet (1743-1781). He wrote the lyrics to the Danish national anthem.

CPSIA information can be obtained at www.ICGtesting.com
Printed in the USA
BVOW070634150713

325699BV00001B/3/P